TEACHING AND LEARNING ONLINE

A Step-by-Step Guide for Designing an Online K–12 School Program

Shawn Morris

A SCARECROWEDUCATION BOOK

The Scarecrow Press, Inc.
Lanham, Maryland, and Oxford
2002

A SCARECROWEDUCATION BOOK

Published in the United States of America
by Scarecrow Press, Inc.
A Member of the Rowman & Littlefield Publishing Group
4720 Boston Way, Lanham, Maryland 20706
www.scarecroweducation.com

PO Box 317
Oxford
OX2 9RU, UK

British Library Cataloguing in Publication Information Available

Library of Congress Cataloging-in-Publication Data

Morris, Shawn, 1962–
    Teaching and learning online : a step-by-step guide for designing an online K-12
    school program / Shawn Morris.
        p. cm.
    "A Scarecrow Education book."
    Includes bibliographical references and index.
    ISBN 0-8108-4404-4 (alk. paper)—ISBN 0-8108-4403-6 (pbk. : alk. paper)
    1. Instruction systems—Design. 2. Computer-assisted instruction. 3. Internet
in education. 4. Distance education. I. Title.

LB1028.38 .M67 2002
371.33'4—dc21

                                                    2002070564

⊗™ The paper used in this publication meets the minimum requirements of
American National Standard for Information Sciences—Permanence of Paper for
Printed Library Materials, ANSI/NISO Z39.48-1992.
Manufactured in the United States of America.

To all the Wichita Public School personnel who made
Wichita eSchool a reality.
My love and thanks for time to write this book to
Don, Chris, and Tyler

CONTENTS

PREFACE

Getting into the business of online teaching and learning for K–12 education is a huge undertaking. It is not for the faint of heart. This book takes you through the planning and implementation of creating the online program we developed for home school students in our Midwestern community. Your district and program needs may not be the same as ours, but many of the same processes will need to be completed to get your online program up and running.

Planning for and designing our online program was one of the hardest yet most fulfilling experiences of my teaching career. Projects like this take a lot of dedication and neverending hours of time. Your online program will be new and innovative, but you need to make sure that those involved in the project are visionary and have unending enthusiasm for what the program can be. By its very nature, *online* also means that the program will never be complete. Creating courses online allows you to assess and alter parts of your program on a daily basis. It is a continuous project that will stretch every educator who is exposed to it. Our program was something that not only stretched the district's vision about teaching and learning, but also many of the teachers who were involved with creating, mentoring, and teaching courses online.

The process is not a step-by-step progression so much as it is a multi-layered development that involves working in many areas simultaneously. The most effective way to create an online school from scratch is to multitask and work on many areas at once. I would suggest that you have one person who has his or her fingers in all the pies, who has a pulse on all areas of the program you are creating. This one person doesn't have to have skills in every area but should be the one who holds all the elements together and can tell the whole story of what you are all about and what you are trying to accomplish. This person needs to be able to network within your organization, to understand when expert help is needed, and to be able to work with the experts in different departments to get what is needed for your program. Although this coordinator will wear many hats, he or she does not have to be an expert in all areas. This person can't be an island, but instead must be a bridge to join together many departments in your school district to create your online program. I am that point person for the Wichita Public School's Wichita eSchool online program. As point person and coordinator of our program, I attempt to guide you step-by-step through the creation process in this book.

❶

COORDINATOR OF
THE ONLINE PROGRAM

I was selected as the coordinator for our district's online program because of my varied background in education. I have always had a love of teaching with technology. I have a background in library, elementary, middle, and high school teaching and technology training of children as well as adults. My background was well rounded for designing an online program but in no way limited or defined the credentials that an educator could bring to a coordinator position. I don't think you could create the perfect job description for a project like this. The list of duties in this chapter is by no means all-inclusive. The bullet "Perform other duties related to . . . " at the end of the following list covers the duties that will come up as implementation actually starts to happen. There is no effective way to plan for every contingency that may occur. It is important to find a coordinator who has vision and is flexible enough to keep everything moving along as the program changes and grows. That said, here are a few points to consider when hiring for the coordinator position.

DUTIES OF ONLINE PROGRAM COORDINATOR

- Make and implement decisions and purchasing for hardware, software, hosting of website, and curriculum needs for the program

- Select, train, and monitor all teaching staff
- Maintain and keep open communication channels with district staff and the community
- Plan and design all standards for teachers to follow in course format and content
- Monitor curriculum development and coordinate instructional programs
- Plan and control program budget
- Plan, schedule, and communicate all student activities online and onsite
- Work with communication and marketing departments in developing informational and promotional information
- Plan and implement enrollment process
- Order and distribute equipment, textbooks, and supplemental materials
- Facilitate team planning and teacher, parent/student, and other resource group meetings
- Coordinate with other departments and administrators within the district
- Perform other duties related to designing and implementing the online program as needed

Coordinator as Point Person

If the person selected to lead the online program doesn't have some of the abilities listed above, his job will be to find those people in the district who can handle the duties. The coordinator needs to stay in the loop, however, and always be privy to major decisions and changes in the program in order to be up to speed; he or she is the spokesperson for the program in every aspect. I can't reiterate enough how important it is for one person to be the point person for the online program. Teaching and learning online is so new for most school personnel and the community that one person needs to be the person to come to for the definitive answer to questions about the program. It only confuses people to have different people giving them different answers. When starting something this new and creative, it takes a lot of communication. Unfortunately, there will already be a lot of miscommunication coming from uninformed factions within and outside your organization. Everyone needs one person to come to for the ultimate answer to questions about online school programs. If the coordinator doesn't have a ready answer, he or she can then go through channels to later provide the answer.

Working Relationship with Top-Level Administrators

The coordinator for the program needs to be in direct communication with top-level administrators in the district. The administrators at that level are able to move in different circles within the district, in the community, and at the state level. This connection will be invaluable to the program. Top-level administrators are able to open doors and create opportunities that the coordinator wouldn't be able to accomplish alone. Partnering with a top-level administrator provides legitimacy to the coordinator and the program that couldn't be accomplished without the administrator's blessing. This relationship is key and needs to be nurtured. The top-level administrator needs to be in the loop for any program elements that he or she may need to know about in order to present the program in a positive light wherever he or she may go. This person can help streamline the decision process and can get others in the district to work for the online program. He or she has clout within the district that can definitely help if the coordinator gets in a bind and needs assistance or support from others within the organization. Top-level administrators also have the ear of board of education members, state officials, and other community members who can make or break the online program.

In my case, our district deputy superintendent is the top-level administrator with whom I work hand-in-hand to create and expand our online program. Not only does he have a strong vision for online teaching and learning, but also feels that this program is worth his time and effort. I don't have to go through layers of people to get to him when I need advice or help making district-level decisions for the program. He is an integral part of the program and its strongest supporter. The professional relationship with a top-level administrator on a regular basis has also allowed me to learn about the inner workings of the district I've worked for during the last eighteen years. I now understand how the district works as a whole, and that information has been invaluable in knowing how decisions get made and where to go for assistance in different departments as the design and implementation of the program takes place. I will add one caveat to this relationship: this administrator should be in the know about the program and even attend planning meeting when possible, but the day-to-day decisions for the program should be made by the coordinator. The administrator can't be available on a daily basis to make those decisions. The best relationship would be one where the administrator doesn't micromanage the coordinator and the coordinator doesn't defer all decision making to the administrator. There needs to be a balance of support, communication, and ownership for both the administrator and the coordinator.

2

DETERMINING YOUR AUDIENCE

Designing online classes requires gearing your program for a small audience; to initially target online classes for K–12 students is too large an audience. You need to narrow to a specific audience or group of audiences that will allow you to create your classes with that audience in mind. Some of the possible audiences include homebound students, expelled students, dropouts, pregnant students and/or those who are new parents, students who have failed courses, advanced placement students, students currently attending brick-and-mortar sites who also want to take a course or two online, summer school those, students who simply want to supplement classes taught face-to-face at schools, or home school students. You need to look at what you want your online program to accomplish. If you are looking at adding online information and communication to enhance your current brick-and-mortar school classes, you design a completely different program from a program that includes complete courses online.

AUDIENCE OPTIONS

Homebound Students

In most school districts across the country, students who are injured or unable to attend school because of a mental or physical illness are homebound and receive services at home. This usually requires a teacher, not necessarily one who teachers the student's grade level or course subject, to go to the student's home once a week and provide teaching services. This option was probably one of the best that districts could offer before online learning became available. With online learning, however, it is now possible to provide homebound students with a better option in delivering educational materials and instruction. Homebound students often have good and bad days, days when they are getting over a chemotherapy treatment or are taking pain medication to relieve injury, aches, and pains. With the old drop-in scenario, the teacher might have been scheduled to come to a student's home on days or times that the student wasn't in a state of mind to concentrate on learning.

In our district, the homebound teachers were the teachers (usually one from each school) who volunteered, with supplemental pay, to bring schoolwork to any homebound students from their school during the school year. This meant that the teacher was usually an expert in teaching one grade level in elementary or one curriculum area at the middle or high school level. This one teacher shouldn't be expected to know all curriculum areas in all grade levels.

With online classes for homebound students, we are now able to provide lessons and activities created by grade-level and course-area certified teachers. The students have a teacher online to mentor them as they work through assignments created by the course creation teacher. The student is able to log on to the website at any time that is convenient, twenty-four hours a day, seven days a week. If the student is feeling better at midnight, he can log on and start working. The student isn't tied to one specific date and time for the big visit from the assigned homebound teacher.

An online supplement provides the homebound teachers with a wealth of lessons and activities that they don't have to research and create. The online teacher would have all those lessons ready for use wherever the student left off when he or she quit attending school because of illness. When the student improves to the point where he or she is ready to return to school, he or she could be right on target if the same curriculum and textbooks used in the brick-and-mortar schools are used for the online programs.

Expelled Students

When students are expelled from our district schools for as much as one full school year, their education is often put on hold because they are a serious risk to the safety of others. We provide educational opportunities through a partnership with an area boys' and girls' center. If your district is looking for a way to assist expelled students in continuing their educations, you could provide online courses that students could access from their homes or libraries. An even better solution might be to provide online lessons for a community center to access. That way, the wayward student would have positive role models and assistance from the community center staff who are there to help the student get back on track. Community center staff might lack the skills to create and teach courses, but online courses would provide that service. The other students and staff at your schools are safe, and the expelled student can continue his or her education, which may help turn his or her life around.

Dropouts

Dropouts in every community often have a desire to return to school to finish their education. Creating an online program for dropouts is one way to deal with the age of some of these dropouts. Sometimes they are not just fresh out of school but are older adults who would like finishing their coursework. Often, these students wouldn't fit into a regular highschool atmosphere. These older students might work full time, which means that they need a more flexible program. Online learning is just that. Students can work a forty-hour week and still steadily work through their online courses. Online courses provide a perfect solution for many dropouts' schedules and lifestyles.

One issue you need to consider with dropout students, as well as for expelled students and those who have failed a course at least once, is that they are often not high-achieving students. They have special needs that must be addressed, and you might need to provide a schedule of check-up assistance to keep these students on track. You also might need to assist these students in learning how to organize their work time in order to be successful.

Pregnant Students and/or New Parents

Even though our district provides day care within our high schools for new student parents so they can continue their education, quite a few new mothers and pregnant girls take advantage of our online program. Many of the girls in our online program are mothers who had dropped out of school once their children were born because it was just too hard to schedule child care, transportation, working, and schoolwork into their lives. Online courses allow new mothers to work on courses when their children are sleeping, which may very well be late into the night or early in the morning. Public schools allow pregnant girls to continue to attend classes, but sometimes the girls have issues with other students harassing them, with morning sickness, or with other complications common in teenage pregnancies. An online program allows these girls to work when it is most convenient for them, in a less stressful atmosphere.

These students are usually more conscientious than dropout students or expelled students. They sometimes fall behind in coursework due to time spent with their children, but as a group, they have a strong desire to finish their education and better themselves for their futures, as well as for their children.

Students Who Have Failed Courses

Another audience for online courses are the students who have failed courses at least once in your brick-and-mortar schools. All schools must deal with students who fail one or more courses. These students often take the same courses again, taught by the very same teachers. Nothing really changes, and they often fail the courses for a second time. As an alternative to this scenario, you could provide an online opportunity to complete courses and receive credit. You need to tailor your online program toward students who most likely aren't good at organizing their work or managing their time well. These skills need to be taught along with course content. Regular check-ins and face-to-face mentoring sessions could help you assist these students as they attempt to take online courses. In many cases, getting these students away from the influences of other students in school buildings allows them to give the curriculum the time they need to in order to finish assignments and receive course credit. Online courses also give these low-achieving students a different venue for taking their courses. We have found that using the computers to take courses is something many students enjoy because they choose to work with computers in their leisure time. An online program also allows a customized learning program for each individual student. They don't have to try keep up with a pace in a classroom that is too fast for them. This type of learning allows the students to slow down if needed and to work on concepts until they master them and are ready to move on.

Advanced Placement Students

This audience for an online program is different from most of the other students. As a rule, these students are self-motivated and organized. They are sometimes so involved in school activities and are taking so many college-bound core courses that they don't have time in their day to take everything they would like to take. Offering advanced placement courses online would give these students an opportunity to take some courses on a self-paced basis at home after school hours. These students wouldn't need all the organizational assistance other audiences would need. They want all the information and materials available to them so they can just do the work. Being able to pace the work to their individual learning speeds would be a real plus for these students because they wouldn't be held back by slower students. This is a great way to offer advanced placement classes in all subject areas for all students. Not all high schools have advanced placement teachers in all subject areas. Online advanced placement levels the playing field for all students in a district and affords them the opportunity to take advanced placement courses in all subject areas.

In conjunction with the advanced placement courses, a district could also provide other high-level online courses that are difficult to offer at all district schools. As teachers become scarce, the availability of teachers qualified to teach these courses may dwindle. Consequently, being able to offer these advanced courses to students may become a problem. Online is one way to provide higher-level and advanced placement courses in an equitable way for all students.

Students Attending Brick-and-Mortar Schools

You could also choose to add online courses as an option for students in your current schools. You could offer a wide variety of courses similar to those already offered at sites, with the online program just being another learning option for students. This is a way to equitably provide courses for all students. Many elective courses are not offered at all of the sites in a school district. A website would be a way to offer courses to students who attend schools where there are no teachers qualified to teach those courses. You can give the students an opportunity to have a real expert teaching their courses and offer every student the best learning opportunities available in your district.

One idea for these courses is to offer the online courses and allow students to work from home in the evenings but also provide a lab where students can go on a daily or weekly basis to check in, get help, and turn in assignments. This is a hybrid approach for using online classes in conjunction with face-to-face assistance and mentoring.

Summer School

Online courses could be an option for students who need to repeat a course because of failure during the regular school year or as a way to take enrichment classes. Not all summer school classes would work online, but many of them could. Drivers' education text and written work could even be online, but online course work would need to be combined with actual driving practice in a car with an instructor. With so many students needing remedial summer school courses, some districts find it hard to also provide enrichment opportunities in the summer. Online instruction is one way to provide a variety of options to allow students to keep learning during the summer and to try a different way to learn. Often, the summer school schedule is such that the students need to attend for only half the day. This can be difficult for some working parents to do on a daily basis. Transportation is an issue for summer classes at schools but not for online classes because students can work right from their homes.

Supplement for Face-to-Face Classes

This option is not a true online program. In this option, courses that are taught at schools have supplements for their classes available online. Your online site is a place to store course worksheets, project directions, calendars for assignment due dates, testing information, help and tip sheets, communications with parents, forms, syllabi, grades, and other information. Students are able to access these documents and information online at school or at home. If students need a worksheet or form, the teacher doesn't have to be the one responsible for getting a copy to the students. The responsibility is now put on the students, who can access what they need online.

This option allows parents to be involved in what is happening in classes at school. They are kept in the communication loop. They can check when assignments are due, check student grades on a daily basis, and be a partner with the teaching staff in helping their children succeed. Everything that is happening in classes becomes very public when you supplement classes online. You also provide students with a way to access materials they need from home on weekends, evenings, when they are ill, or during holidays.

Home School Students

In Dowling's article "The Learning Place," she stated that 2 million children are now being taught at home in the United States.[1] This number is increasing by 15 percent a year. As more and more families choose to educate their children at home, more and more options will be available to meet their teaching and learning needs.

During the 1980s, evangelical Christians wanting to control their children's exposure to mainstream culture initiated some of the first movements toward home schooling. In the 1990s, school violence frightened more parents into joining the home school ranks. As more students are taught individually at home, changes in how we teach take place. Peggy Farber described in her article "The Face of Home-schooling" how public schools are left scrambling to find ways to supplement their dwindling revenues as more students are home schooled.[2] One solution is a public school–home school partnership. Some of the programs for home school students are classes and special projects offered at brick-and-mortar schools. Other programs from public schools involve offering online curriculum and teachers assisting families online. Public schools in the past were very reluctant to work with home school families, but this is not the case today. Online schools are definitely a trend in the early twenty-first century.

The intended audience in my district for our online courses was originally the home school students who had left public education. We knew home schooling was a growing trend nationally and would continue to be a trend both nationally and locally. We also knew that many of those students who were being home schooled would return to public schools sometime during their K–12 education years. Most home school students only home school for a short time. This often means that students come back to our classrooms behind in some or all curriculum areas. Even if parents were very conscientious about teaching at home, they often left out teaching some of our district objectives. We wanted the home school students to be up to speed with what their grade-level peers were doing in school and wanted them to be exposed to the same learning objectives. This turned out to be something that home school parents really liked about our program. They were finally aware of the district and state objectives and felt that we had provided a real and tangible way for them to compare their children working at home to their grade-level peers.

We also found that some parents who were home schooling were not prepared to teach. They lacked skills to teach all subject areas and often didn't realize the time that needed to be spent consistently on a daily basis to complete a year's worth of learning objectives. When parents first saw all the lessons and activities we provided online for all subject areas, they were overwhelmed. Some parents thought that their child had all the reading skills needed if he or she could read library books fluently.

Comprehension and writing activities were often ignored. We also found that even home school students who had good home school teachers often lacked writing skills across the curriculum. Home school students are in a setting on a daily basis where they can verbalize their learning. Consequently, they haven't had practice organizing and writing down their thoughts and findings during learning activities. Most of our home school students could have used more opportunities to practice their writing skills.

We were looking to create a partnership with home school parents. This concept for an online program will not work if it is a dictatorship on the part of the public school district. Home school parents have already made a decision to be a major influence in their children's education. Public schools can't march in and tell parents they are taking over. Offering our assistance and doing so in the least restrictive environment was the secret to our success. At first, parents were very surprised to find their local public school district reaching out to them and their children. For some, we will never be an option; for others, it is a way to teach their children at home but also to get all the lessons, resources, and even related websites for core curriculum areas. To have a certified teacher create the lessons and find appropriate hands-on and electronic resources is a home school parent's dream come true. We do a lot of the background footwork and searching to create a variety of activities that teach grade-level curriculum objectives.

Often students are home schooled because they work slower than the place of an average classroom or because the child isn't challenged in school and spends a lot of time in a structured classroom waiting for others to move on. In both instances, their parents believe their child needs to move at his or her own pace, not the average set in a classroom. Our online program allows this to happen because everything is available at all times, so that a parent can spend more time on an activity or extend learning beyond what would be possible in the hours students spend in school. Flexibility is the real benefit and is the one thing that is so hard to do in a class with thirty students at different learning ability levels. Online allows for individualized education within a framework of learning objectives. It isn't a matter of seat time so much as mastery of learning objectives and performance based on assessing daily progress.

AUDIENCE OBJECTIVES

I have defined for you a variety of audiences for an online program. Something to remember is that you can't be everything to everyone. If your plan is to try reach every one of the audiences I have written about here, you will have a hard time achieving your goals in a way that benefits all audiences. You have enough to do just getting an online program off the ground without biting off too much in the audience department. We started with home school students. In the process of creating our program, other audiences actually found us. We didn't market our program to them but, through word of mouth, calls and e-mails arrived from audiences we hadn't intended to reach. Some of them could easily fit into the program we had created; others were told that what we had just wasn't intended for them and really wouldn't be the best choice for their education.

If you are looking to be a dropout recovery program, you could also cater your program to students who have failed courses. This may be a good combination of audiences who would need similar resources and assistance online. On the other hand, if you combine a program for advanced placement students with your dropout population, you may find it very difficult to effectively create an online program that truly meets both audiences' needs because they are so different in their learning abilities and study skills.

I would also recommend that you start slow and build as you go. You can't create it all in a day. You have enough to do to create an online program that works for just one of these audiences. If you try to create too much, you may lose the quality you need to show your audience as well as the learning community in your area that you have created a program that is well thought out and meets the needs of its intended audience.

NOTES

1. Claudia G. Dowling, "The Learning Place," *People* 55, no. 8 (February 2001), 42–47.

2. Peggy Farber, "The Face of Homeschooling," *Harvard Education Letter* 17, no. 2 (March/April 2001), 1–3.

3

DEVELOPING AND SHARING YOUR VISION

DEVELOPING YOUR VISION

Once you have a person coordinating the planning, designing, and launching of your online program and you have defined your audience(s), your next step is to develop a vision for your online program and to share that vision with all your stakeholders. You need to define for everyone just what the intentions are for your online program. If you can't define what your online program is about, others will never figure out what you hope to accomplish.

After we determined our initial audience for our online program, defining a vision was a fairly simple process. We knew that our goal was to eliminate barriers between public schools and home school families. Therefore, our vision became: "Wichita eSchool's mission is to eliminate barriers between home school and traditional school-based learning by offering lessons, resources, and teaching support."

Once you have your audience defined and know what you are going to try to accomplish, your vision should be rather easy to create. It may take some time, though, to think about what is needed and how an online program might be the best way to achieve your goals.

Once the vision is defined, don't just leave it as a vision written in stone, never to be altered for any reason. By virtue of being an online curriculum, your program can be fluid and everchanging. Our original vision is already in need of an overhaul in year two of construction. We are reaching more audiences than just home school students at this time. Our vision has moved beyond our original intentions and goals. We need to redefine who we are and what we are about. Redefining our vision allows everyone within the program to examine his or her work and personal goals. This is a positive activity for any growing organization. It allows everyone involved to step back from the day-to-day mundane duties and look a little deeper into what the program is about and how they each fit into that vision.

Any time staff loses their focus on what your online program is trying to accomplish, your program vision can be one of the things that should refocus them and help them get back on track with renewed commitment to the program's cause. If the vision fails to do that, then it might be an indication that you need to revisit the vision, or it could be that that person is no longer committed to the vision and needs to move on to other projects.

SHARING YOUR VISION

Once a vision is created for any endeavor, it needs to be shared with all stakeholders. Many of the stakeholders may be involved in defining the vision, but even if they aren't part of the original vision-defining process, all stakeholders need to be informed of the vision and then kept up-to-date as the vision changes with time. Some stakeholders for our online program are the same ones you would find in any town or city. They include the local board of education, state legislature and state education personnel, representatives from the local teachers' unions, staff members from the school, district administrators, and the public, which includes students and their parents. All of these stakeholders are important to the success of every online program in one way or another. Some of these stakeholders have the power to make or break an online program. Other stakeholders are your intended audience; if they aren't informed about the program and its vision, you may be creating something that no one will use.

Local Board of Education

It is vitally important to have your local board of education involved
with the creation of an online program. This is where your top-level administrator will be invaluable. The board needs to receive background
information about the possibility of creating an online program. They
need to buy into the idea early on or you will most likely find that they
will put obstacles in your way every time you come to them for funding
or permission to expand your program. It may be that your board members are visionary and can see where online education is moving in both
higher education and in K–12 education nationally. The board of education for Wichita Public Schools is very visionary and has been since
the very beginning. If your board isn't quite as visionary as ours, it will
be up to you and your top-level administrators to educate them about
the possibilities of online education for your district. These benefits
might include increasing student funding from the state in order to educate students not currently enrolled in your schools, increasing communications with parents, increasing technology skills for the teaching
staff involved in the program, or even being a futuristic district that is
willing to look beyond the four walls of traditional schools to educate the
local population. This list is by no means complete. You need to research
your own local area to find benefits to share with your board. What I
have found is that boards are people who give of their own time to public education; as a group, they believe that options and choices are all a
part of what public education should be about.

State Legislature and Other State Education Personnel

In order to get state funding for our students in Kansas, we have different ways to count students. For our online program students, we
chose to use the September 20 attendance day counting method. Our
online students need to spend September 20 at one of the district's
sites. We use our Instructional Support Center, which is where the online school office is located. By having the students attend on this date,
we are able to receive state full-time equivalency (FTE) funding for
each student. In order to be able to receive this funding, we needed to
be able to demonstrate to the state finance personnel that our online
program was in fact a program that very closely followed classes at our

regular school sites. We also had to show that teacher support was always available to students.

Once the idea of online programs started to crop up in different areas around our state, the state commissioner and the deputy commissioner of education created a committee to set the criteria that all Internet-based programs must adhere to. Besides the criteria that students attend a site on September 20 for FTE counting, online students are required to take state and district assessments; certified teachers must be available to the online students; and records must be kept of the amount of time students spend on coursework. If a school district can't meet these criteria, it is not allowed to count Internet-based students for state funding.

There are already a handful of online programs open for business in Kansas. The state legislature is currently looking at the quality of what is being offered online. Some districts are feeling the pressure from losing students to online programs. No longer do students only have the local schools to get their educations; they are able to look at online programs to meet their educational needs. Online education by definition can be anywhere, anytime. Local school districts now have to compete with other programs for their student funding dollars. We have yet to see in our state how this will play out. In commercial enterprises, competition lifts everyone to a higher level of products and services. If this holds true in education, the students will benefit from the competition for their patronage.

I get calls on a regular basis from legislative fact finders who have requests to get answers to questions about what we are doing online. I am always more than happy to share what we are all about when asked. I tell them to call any time they need information. I know there can be a lot of misinformation floating around about online programs. When anyone from the state has called to ask questions, our goal is to pass along a very positive feeling about our online program and our intentions to help students learn.

When you start your online program, you need to get in contact with your state legislature and state officials in your department of education. These people need to know what you are doing, and they may need to be educated about what online programs can accomplish for students in your state. If you don't have any other online programs in your state, you will be the trend setter in establishing this type of program for students.

This will mean a lot of dialogue. If you have a quality program and have really thought through how you will assist students, the benefits of an online program will be obvious to state officials when you share your vision and goals.

This is definitely an area where your top-level administrator will be of great importance. He or she will already have communication channels established and will be invaluable in communicating with people from your state department and legislature.

Local Teachers' Unions

Your local teachers' unions definitely need to be kept in the communication loop. They are charged with protecting your district's teachers from unfair labor practices. As such, they want to assure their teachers (and themselves) that your program isn't taking advantage of the teachers involved in the program. They want to know that you are compensating your teachers for their time and efforts. This means that you need to look at other compensation packages within your district to find one that is in line with what would be expected for the work the teachers are being asked to do in your online program.

In our case, we have meetings with the union president and other union officials to share our vision and goals. They see that we are compensating our teachers at a rate that is equitable for the project. We work very closely with our teaching and creation staff to make sure that the pay they receive makes it worth their time to want to continue with the program.

It is worth it in the long run to compensate your teachers well so they don't feel put upon and spend their time and energy complaining about the amount of work they must do for the small amount of compensation they are receiving. If that happens, it won't take long for the union personnel to get wind of the complaints and step in to fight for the teachers.

District Administration

Even though you have kept your district superintendents up to date about your online program, you need to get the word out to other central

administrators. Meeting with curriculum directors, assistant superintendents, and other district-level personnel to share your vision and goals is
important for many reasons. First and foremost, these are the people who
will support you and your online program when needed. These people are
also able to get the word out about what your program is about by sharing
your information with the personnel in their departments. You can't talk
individually to everyone in your district, so reaching district-level administrators is a good start in spreading the word. If district-level personnel
aren't in your communication loop or have misinformation about your online program, you may not be able to successfully communicate your vision to the district as a whole.

District Staff

In a large district, effective communication can be an enormous endeavor. There are a lot of people to try and reach, and it is imperative
that you reach as many of them as possible. All of the people who work
in your district can become marketing agents. If they know what your
online program is all about, they will be able to share that information
with people they come into contact with outside your district. If they
aren't in the communication loop and don't understand your vision, they
could become agents of misinformation. If people within your own in-
stitution are agents of misinformation, your job of communicating to the
public will be that much harder to accomplish. These are your colleagues and friends. They should know what you are trying to accomplish, even if it takes a lot of time and effort on your part to accomplish
this goal. Counselors at schools are a district staff group that definitely
needs to know about your online program and its intended audience.
They are often the people students come to when they are in search of
alternative educational options.

Members of the Public

Ultimately, you need to communicate your vision and goals to the
public. This is where you get your clientele. There are many ways to
market your online program to its intended audience(s). First, you need
to prepare some written materials that can be passed out at any gather-

ing you may attend where people might be interested in your program. This puts contact information in their hands so that they can get in touch with you at a later date if they have further interest in your program. We created flyers our first year and made fifty-page catalogs for our second year. We found that most of the calls and e-mail questions were basically asking the same questions repeatedly. It made sense to create a catalog that answered many of those questions in writing so that people could contact us only when they needed more details. It saved a lot of time during enrollment for the second year. We were growing and just couldn't spend the time to conduct one-hour informational phone calls with each and every family who was interested in our program. We mailed the flyers and catalogs to any family who called or e-mailed with interest in the program. We also send out a large mailing each year to all families who resister with the state board of education as home school families. This is where we really pinpointed our specific audience and tried to get marketing information in their hands.

Another good resource for getting the word out to the public is your local newspaper or television news program. Our online program was innovative and newsworthy enough in the beginning to generate interest from the news media in and of itself. Whenever I had to speak at the board of education meetings, which are televised, the news stations often showed our segment of the meetings in their nightly programs. Our local newspaper periodically wrote about our online program during the initial creation year. We never had to seek out the news media to cover our stories, but it would be a good idea to work with your district communications and marketing department to keep the media informed of developments in your program and to help generate interest if it isn't originally there.

In our district, we have a local cable station dedicated to school district programming. This was another source of getting information out to the public. I was amazed at how many people told me they heard about our program when they were watching cable TV at 2:00 in the morning. If you have a school cable station, it would certainly be a great idea to tap into that media to share your vision and goals with the public.

Because your program will be an online one, it makes sense to have an informational website to market your product to the public. This is where people can go to get information similar to the information they would receive in a catalog. All the information (the vision, goals, intended audience, program components, contact information, etc.) should be available on the website. We also provide a form that can be filled out and submitted to our offices online for pre-enrollment purposes. This gives us information like mailing addresses, names, ages, and e-mail addresses so we can send pre-enrolled students additional information and make contact on a personal basis. Whenever we receive a pre-enrollment online, we make a point of calling the family and introducing ourselves to put a more personal feel to our program.

Another source of marketing our online program turned out to be our end-of-year open house. We invite our current families to attend and to allow students to share the learning projects they completed during the year and celebrated with a kindergarten, fifth-grade, eighth-grade, and senior graduation cake. Local home school families, their friends, and relatives are invited to attend. I spend part of the evening giving a brief talk to anyone interested in joining our program, and we generate quite a few new students. This method of marketing is a very casual approach and is partly successful because of the positive word-of-mouth testimonies from current families. They bring in their friends and neighbors to see what our program is all about. You can't ask for a better endorsement of a program than to have current users praising what it has done for their children.

You need to devote both time and money to marketing your online program. This is a new way to educate students and, as such, will take effort to get the information out to the public. You also need to know that marketing needs to start happening even before the courses are created. You have to believe that if you create it, they will come. That takes a real leap of faith and can be scary when you aren't even sure what the end product will look like. You can market your vision, goals, and the premise behind your online program, as parents are acceptable of some ambiguity in the beginning. Just remember that you need to be able to answer most of the families' questions. You can let them know that you will research and get back to them as soon as you do have an answer to any questions for which you don't have a ready answer.

4

SECURING FUNDING
AND BUILDING A BUDGET

FUNDING

Even though you are working within a school district that is funded by tax dollars, you may need to think of your online program as a new program for funding through grant funds. I say this in reference to how to develop an initial operating budget. You need to purchase equipment and pay teachers before you actually create any funding source if you are using any state FTE funds. In our case, we used grant money for innovative new projects as seed money to get started. After the first state attendance day, our program became self-funded. Grants are a great way to get money that is often hard to come by in regular operating budgets in any school district. Federal technology grants are a good place to start looking for the kinds of funds you need to get started. Your state may also have grant opportunities for innovative technology programs. Starting an online teaching program is still an innovative idea, so you will have a good chance of securing start-up funding through grant money.

Although grants are an excellent idea for start-up funding, they won't work for long-term funding of your program. Most grants have a lifespan of one to five years. Once the grant funding time expires, you will be left with no funding source to continue your program. You need to find hard money that will allow you to continue your program year to year. In Kansas, online programs are able to collect FTE funds for students attending school online if we follow all the state's guidelines for Internet-based programs. You should look into this option in your state as a funding source.

Another hard-money source would be to add your program into your district's general fund budget. Once you prove the validity of your online program, it might be successful enough to become just another part of how your district does business. I believe that general fund budgets are strapped in all districts across the nation, but I also believe that some items budgeted for in the past (like textbooks, reference books, and nonfiction research library books) will soon be replaced with online versions that can be updated instantly. Funds will need to be reallocated to online resource services, but you might be able to include your online program budget into the technology dollars coming from obsolete items in the district. This is just one idea to pursue. You will have to research the budget needs in your district to find some creative ways to include new and innovative uses for technology in your general district budget.

BUDGETING

Your budget requirements will be driven by what type of online program you are designing, but you will have some basic areas to consider as you create the operating budgets for your startup (see table 4.1) and continuation years (see table 4.2). The upfront money is daunting, but once startup is accomplished, the operating budget does decrease. Part of the

Table 4.1.   Sample Startup Budget

Budget Item	Cost
Marketing	$5,500.00
Computers/Hardware/Software	$175,000.00
Platform/Web hosting/Tech support	$37,000.00
Office supplies/Workbooks	$12,500.00
Personnel	$180,000.00
Total Expenses	$410,000.00

Table 4.2.   Sample Continuation Years Operating Budget

Budget Item	Cost
Marketing	$5,000.00
Computers/Hardware/Software	$230,000.00
Platform/Web hosting/Tech support	$40,000.00
Office supplies/Workbooks	$15,000.00
Personnel	$300,000.00
Total Expenses	$590,000.00

reason for this, at least in our case, is the money dedicated to paying teachers to create their courses. It costs more money to pay teachers to create courses than it does to pay teachers to supplement, maintain, and enhance courses in subsequent years.

Startup Budget

Personnel, like any program or school in your district, is your biggest expense. Your full-time personnel need to be paid their salaries as well as all their benefits. In our case, this only includes the coordinator of the program and a secretary. As your program grows, you may find the need to add other support staff. These positions might include a counselor to assist students in choosing courses, a technical support person to troubleshoot computer issues and assist everyone in using the technology, and even temporary staff during enrollment time when you may need extra help to handle a variety of things.

If teachers work during the summer or evenings as a supplemental assignment, they need additional pay for their time. We often pay teachers who work after hours by the hour, but with a project like designing an online course, paying teachers by the hour was not the way to go. I asked teachers to track their creation time and found out that the teachers who already had very organized curriculum and lessons and those with the most computer skills were very quick in designing courses. On the other hand, those teachers who were not as organized coming into the project were taking large amounts of time to create their courses. Although I made sure all teachers had the technology skills they needed, teachers who weren't strong users of technology before joining our program found the process to be time consuming. Some of the best designers of online courses were the ones who would have received the least amount of money if we had paid them by the hour.

An alternate way to pay your teachers for creating their courses is by giving all of them the same amount of compensation. With this option, all the teachers know that they will receive the same amount; if they spend a lot more time than their counterparts, it is up to them to find the time needed to finish their courses by the deadline. The teachers in our program felt this was a fair way to pay everyone for their creation time. Part of the money the teachers in our program received for course creation was the time they spent in the two-week workshop where they learned about the technology, planned with each other, and got started designing their courses with me right there to assist them. When they left the workshop, they knew they had the rest of the summer to finish their courses. To create a course for online students, our teachers received $4,000 and the use of a computer package in their homes.

Teachers also need to be compensated for mentoring their students online. It is not a good idea to just throw a course onto the Internet and not have the teacher who designed it available to answer questions and help students find assignment elements. This pay is not as easy to figure out. In our case, we staggered the pay for mentoring to reflect the time teachers at different levels had to devote to online students.

Elementary school teachers   Our elementary teachers designed all curriculum areas they teach in their schools. They were paid an extra $1,000 to mentor students and parents online. We found that the bulk of online questions were during the first month of the school year when everyone was new navigating the courses. After that time, the volume of e-mail questions decreased, and teachers were only occasionally asked questions. Although teachers don't spend a lot of time e-mailing, we wanted to pay them for the fact that they need to check their e-mail daily and to be on call when needed.

Middle school teachers   Because our middle school teachers only designed one subject area course each, they were paid $500 to mentor their courses. Each family then had four core teachers to act as resources, and the teaching load was therefore shared by all four teachers per grade level.

High school teachers   High school was a whole new mentoring scale for us. The teachers in our online program for high school prepare and assign all weekly assignments, grade the work, give semester finals, and give assessments. These teachers needed to be paid for the equivalent of taking on an extra class. We also knew that some of the courses would have twenty-five to thirty-five students and others would only have five to six students. The teachers were compensated using a staggered pay scale that ranged from $1,500 for smaller classes up to $3,500 for larger classes. We found that the larger class sizes tended to be the freshman classes. When creating an online program, you may find that your program will grow to the higher grade levels as your freshman move up through the program.

Technology Equipment, Software, and Platforms

One of the first technology decisions to make for an online program is what online e-learning platform to use to create your courses. There are a variety of e-learning platforms on the market to choose from. You will need to look at functionality, ease of use by teachers, technical support, and ultimately the cost to purchase and renew the contract every year. This decision is a big one. Once you start training your teachers and designing courses on one platform, it is extremely difficult for both teachers and students to switch to another platform. Look for a platform that has some staying power; you don't want to get into the predicament of the online company closing shop and leaving you hanging. It is worth the extra money to deal with a more established company just for the peace of mind it will bring knowing that the company will be there for the life of your program. Also, be aware that most of the e-learning platforms are designed with university and college users in mind. They sometimes offer a whole university campus and community program that is more than a K–12 program would need or use. This is an ongoing expense for your online program, so make sure you are able to sustain the cost of the platform you select on a yearly basis.

Part of purchasing the e-learning platform is the purchase of technical support. If you are going to use the program for whole courses online or plan to allow teachers throughout your district to supplement their classes online, you will need a higher level of technical support. No one in your district knows the e-learning platform like the company's own technical support staff does. To save time and provide quick and accurate support, it is worth it to purchase a higher level of technical support than it is to purchase the basic level of support.

Once you decide which e-learning platform to purchase, you need to decide where you will house the server that will hold your online software. You have three choices: (1) Pay the e-learning company extra money to also provide server services. This option means that the experts for the product upload and update your system. They will have the best understanding of the platform and will get the fixes and patches before any other server service could provide them. (2) Provide the server for your online program within your district. To do this, you need someone with strong server skills who is willing to learn the e-learning platform. This person needs to work closely with the technical support people who work for the e-learning platform so he or she is able to fix patch issues and update new versions of the product. (3) Outsource the service to another company. This option does not provide the most expert technical support, but many server services have well-trained technical personnel who work well with the e-learning technical staff. For all three options, you need technical support for the server at all times, day or night, because when it is down, your program is not available to your students. This is another service that will be an annual renewal contract for your program. Money needs to be set aside in your operating budget on an annual basis. One point to remember when you are contracting with any server services or doing it in-house is the storage and backup of your online program. If the server crashes and you don't have sufficient back-ups, your online program is gone. It is worth the money to have a reliable back-up system.

Another decision you must make regarding the design of your courses is if you are going to design all your courses from scratch or purchase commercial products that provide lessons for students and incorporate them into your program. There are pros and cons to doing this. On the pro side, it is quick and easy because the product is already created. Buying canned curriculum may also save you some money in teachers' compensations, yet that money will only be diverted to the online curriculum purchase. In the beginning, it may appear that purchasing curriculum is cheaper, but renewal of the services and increases in cost may make this choice more expensive over time. Although all online commercial curriculum products claim they teach all state standards, we found that this just wasn't true in many cases. In trying to provide curriculum to meet all fifty state standards, a commercial curriculum may not hone in on your state's specific standards. We believe that designing our own courses provides that one-on-one correlation to both district and state standards. No commercial product can provide lessons that correlate to specific district standards and work seamlessly with your district textbooks. Another point that drew us to designing our own curriculum was that our teachers know their courses inside out because they designed them. They can answer any questions about the course and can locate any and all elements when students and parents need assistance. When you use commercial curriculum, your teachers may not know the courses as intimately and their mentoring support may not be as comprehensive.

We decided that we needed to add video instruction to our courses. This decision wasn't made until the second year when we added high school math courses and found that it was almost impossible to explain in writing how to understand new math concepts. We purchased three video creation one-piece units called Tegrity. These carts each held a CPU, whiteboard annotation camera, instructor camera, and document camera. Without a lot of video editing expertise, the teachers were able to create videos where they could speak to the online students, point to bulleted information on a PowerPoint presentation that students could see, and even write on the whiteboard to explain new concepts step-by-step. Our package cost $50,000 for three carts, six months of server service, technical support, upgrades, and two days of training. You could create an online program without the videos, but it really enhanced our program and brought the teachers right into the students' homes. If I had known about the product and what the teachers would do with it, we would have started the first year with the video carts. Now we are playing catch up with the elementary teachers, adding videos after they created their initial courses. It is definitely easier for the teachers to plan for the use of videos as they are creating a new course.

In our program, we provide computers to both teachers and students. We provide the computers to the teachers for use in their homes because that is where they design much of their courses and mentor students online through e-mail communications. This is a perk that all teachers were thrilled about. The teachers not only had the computers in their homes for the online program but for work in their regular classes. We didn't just give the computers to the teachers to own as part of their pay. If they were to own the computers, they would lose district technical support and, over time, the computers would become obsolete and wouldn't be usable for the program. By providing the computers to use as long as a teacher is in the program, we continue with district technical support and provide upgraded computers every year or two. The older computers are then recycled for use in students' homes. This way, the teachers always have the newest technology readily available. We also provided all online teachers with a printer, a scanner, and a cable account at their homes for fast access to the Internet, which is needed for the creation of courses. We originally went with a dial-up Internet service provider (ISP) but found that the dial-up service was too slow and would often hang up on teachers right in the middle of creating tests or lessons. All of the technology placed in the teachers' homes was a benefit that became one of the real draws to joining the online program and staying with it.

Other equipment expenses for our program included the computers, scanners, printers, fax machine, and copier needed in the program office. Because the program was new, we didn't have offices established when we started, so part of our start-up expense was the purchase and set-up of office equipment. This was a one-time expense, although you should trade out older equipment at least every few years to keep the office current with the teachers' technology. During our second year, we also set up an eight-computer learning lab in our offices to allow parents and students to drop in individually for training and to offer a place where students could get help or where they could work quietly away from distractions at home. Setting up a place for students to train or just drop in has been a real asset to the online program and allows us to have some face-to-face interactions with students besides when they come in for finals or state assessments.

Our final computer purchases were for the students who enrolled in our program. This is definitely not something that every online program offers to their students. Our thinking was that we were getting state money to educate our online students and, even with all the other expenses, we had excess money to use in the program. We don't have many of the costs that a brick-and-mortar school would incur, such as lawn mowing services, lunchroom aides, custodial staff, and toilet paper or paper towels, to name a few. The money we save from not having the day-to-day expenses in a building is diverted to technology in our students' homes. We provide a desktop computer that is dial-up and cable modem ready and a printer to print out worksheets and other forms used in the program. For high school students, we also provide a scanner for filling out forms they printed or for hand writing math assignments to send back to teachers for grading. Other assignments are produced through the word processor and handed in through e-mail attachments. The families only get the use of one computer, even if they enroll more than one student. The families only keep the computers for as long as their children are enrolled in our online program. Families must provide their own paper, ink refills, and Internet service providers to access the program online. We have the computers under a three-year warranty contract with the manufacturers and provide technical support through the warranty. We also fix small technical problems through our district technology support department.

A few other issues went into our decision to provide computers to families. One issue was that many of the families who wanted to join our program did not have computers in their homes. Some did not have the income to provide the technology to their children on their own. This is an equity problem that is important to consider. If you choose not to provide computers, your online program will only be available to the haves; the have-nots will not be able to participate. Additionally, we found that if families choose to use their own computers, they often have trouble with the versions of software they have installed and the versions we need them to use in order to access our programs.

Software Purchases

You will need to decide what the teacher and student computer desktops will look like and include. The types of software decisions to make might include what office suite to use for word processing, databases, spreadsheets, and desktop publishing. In our case, we selected Microsoft Office Professional because it was the office suite used everywhere within our district and would be a popular suite on many families' computers. There is no good reason to select a suite other than the one your district uses. You want your online program's software choices to reflect programs already used in your district schools. You want as much crossover of skills as possible for both students and teachers.

Installation of a common browser on all district-purchased computers in your program will assist you down the road when you are troubleshooting browser issues. You also have only one browser to remind teachers and students to upgrade when newer versions are available online. If you use many browsers, it can be time consuming to track all the needed patches, fixes, or upgrades. Access to any online site, however, is not dependent on any one Internet browser.

For scanning documents for global use on the Internet, you need to have the ability to create pdf-formatted documents. This format can be read by anyone on the Internet with a free Adobe Acrobat reader program downloaded from the Internet. We make a point of installing the latest version of Acrobat on all our computers so students don't have to find, download, and install it themselves.

We also chose to add Inspiration software to our teachers' desktops so they had the ability to create graphic organizers for any lessons or for organizational purposes. You have to decide what other software needs your teachers have and provide them the software that allows them to create courses that meet the needs of your program.

You have some decisions to make for your online program computers concerning computer safety issues. You need to install virus protection software on your computers that can be updated regularly through the Internet. Otherwise, the teachers and students have to return their computers to your offices for upgrades. This would be extremely time consuming and a bother to all users. You may also want to consider firewall or filtering software to further protect your equipment from hackers and your students from inappropriate sites.

Once you establish your desktop, you will need to establish standards for your program. If a student plans to use his or her own home computer, you need to have a list of minimum specifications for computer processing speed, memory, Internet browser version, office suite brand and version, plug-in types and versions, and so forth. These standards help use your program at peek efficiency with the least amount of technical issues.

After we purchased and installed all our software and any Internet plug-ins, we created a ghost image of the desktop so that when a computer crashes or is returned and needs to be prepared for a new user, we are able to quickly reinstall the operating system and all the software using just one or two compressed CDs. Without ghosting the desktop, rebuilding each computer would take hours instead of minutes. As each new version of software is available to the public, the ghost images need to be updated so all upgrades happen every time a computer is returned for a rebuild. This way, the computers receive the latest versions of everything when they are ghosted.

Other Supplies

Don't forget to include in your start-up and operating budgets some money for miscellaneous supplies. These supplies might include copier/printer paper, copier toner, ink tanks, CDs, and other basic office supplies. We supply our teaching staff with replacements for printer paper and ink tanks. We do not do the same for the students. There was just no way to monitor the use of printers for only Wichita eSchool uses. Other family members could be using the Wichita eSchool computers for other printing needs. The families are told ahead of time that they have to incur the costs for printing worksheets, lesson directions, and activities, as well as textbook rentals, paper, ink tank replacements, and an ISP service in their homes for Internet service.

We also budgeted for science kits to be checked out by students. These kits contained beakers, test tubes, thermometers, goggles, aprons, and other supplies to conduct experiments. If students lose or break items, they pay replacement costs; otherwise, the use of the kits is free. We did this because it is often easier for us to order in bulk and we can order from supply houses that parents may not have access to. We also purchased sets of novels for English courses and checked them out to students. The students only have to pay for them if they damage or lose them.

Marketing Expenses

There are expenses incurred in marketing an online program. You need to budget for items like brochures, catalogs, letters, postage, envelopes, conference fees, and similar materials and charges. Be aware that you can get a lot of free marketing assistance from local television stations, newspapers, and local and national magazines. Contact your local news departments and let them know about your new online program. Chances are, at least some of them will find the idea worth spotlighting in their education section of the news. After they do an initial piece, you can contact them later with updates on how the program in working, how it is changing, or what new audiences you might have included.

Every time we got free marketing from the press, it always brought in new inquiries about the program. It is important to periodically get the message out to the public as a whole or to a specific group to stir up new interest or connect with people who don't have any idea you are there to offer services. It always helps if you have a positive relationship with news services that are interested in your program and will help you promote it to the public.

CONTINUATION YEARS OPERATING BUDGETS

The start-up budget year will include the most expenses you will encounter in your online program. Many of the expenses in the first year will be one-time expenses. If, however, you are creating your online program a little at a time, your creation costs may continue into years two and three. In our case, we started with elementary courses in year one. We added middle and high school core courses in year two and will add more core and elective courses in year three. The creation pay for teachers continues for all three years and may very well extend into year four as we add more electives to the online program. You may have a small full-time staff in the beginning, but you may need to add more full-time staff in order to meet all the needs of your growing patron base.

Once teachers have created online courses, we pay them to enhance the courses in subsequent years. This means that they are responsible for adding new activities, websites, checking website addresses to make sure they are still available, and a myriad of other things to update and improve their courses. In our case, we paid them one-fourth of the creation pay to enhance their courses in subsequent years. Whenever our district adopts new textbooks in a curriculum area, those teachers are paid half the original creation fee to rewrite the textbook-connected parts of their courses. They still leave the other parts of the courses intact but correlate textbook pages with the activities already online. The textbook did not drive the other activities, so they can still be used. In other words, the courses don't have to be totally scrapped when a new textbook is adopted. Teachers still need to be paid each year for mentoring their online students. This amount may vary depending on the number of students enrolled in courses. As your program grows, the teachers will most likely be paid more to mentor because their class sizes will increase.

Most of the services and contracts that you established during the first year will need to be renewed each year. It would be a good idea to include an additional 5 percent or so in future years to account for increases in renewal costs. Some of the renewal contracts might include any outsourced server services, your e-learning platform, ISP accounts, technical support contracts, and any online curriculum services or databases. Continuation year budgets will also need to include marketing funds and money for consumable office supplies.

As your program grows, you will need to add new teachers to create courses. This means new computers and ISPs for them to create courses, plus their creation pay. As our program increased in student numbers, we also had to purchase more student computers for checkout. Another issue to think about when buying computers is how you plan to phase out older equipment and replace it with newer equipment. This should also be built into your continuation budgets.

5

STAFFING AN ONLINE PROGRAM

TEACHERS

Online teachers can and do come from the pool of teachers working within your district. Your quest in finding the right teachers to teach online is to find those teachers who can transition to different delivery methods. Teachers who are the most popular face-to-face are often the teachers who respond to students' movements, facial expressions, and other gestures and may not necessarily be the best teachers for your online students. Students may respond to these teachers because they joke and laugh with them, pat them on the back, or egg them on to complete tasks. All of these activities are hard to accomplish online. If a teacher uses group dynamics activities in many of his or her classes, they may not translate to the types of group activities you can do online. This is not to say that these teachers can't create dynamic online classes or mentor students online with the same passion they have in a school. Just be aware that some of the dynamics of a face-to-face course may be missing online.

On the other hand, a teacher that students may find boring in school may really be able to soar with an online course. Sometimes these teachers are very meticulous and orderly. This type of teacher many times creates an online class and adds all the little details that make an online course easier to follow. They don't fly by the seat of their pants; their courses are often thorough and don't seem scattered or thrown together. These teachers also may be better at mentoring online than being in a face-to-face class because it is all about content, not gestures and personalities. In other words, your shy or hard-nosed teachers shouldn't be discounted in an online program. Just like the students in online courses, the teachers who are shy or not prone to lengthy talking in class may find a comfort level not found in face-to-face classrooms. They may be more open and bond with students whom they get to know through e-mailing and online chats.

Age and years of teaching experience also fit into the equation when selecting teachers to design online courses. You might think that you should select teachers who are young because they will have the most experience with technology. This may be true, but they may also lack teaching experience and curriculum design skills. I believe I can train the teachers to use the technology needed to create online courses as long as they have the desire to learn the technology. The e-learning platforms on the market today make it so easy; all the teachers need to know is how to fill in boxes with the text they want. Then the teachers just need some additional training for the peripheral software and equipment they will be using.

What is more important than high levels of technology skills is to find teachers who are very familiar with your curriculum and your state and district standards and who can create and write quality lessons. These teachers are probably your more seasoned teachers because they have had many years to perfect their teaching skills and are most familiar with the curriculum and standards. I have found that these teachers were also the most excited as a group to create courses online. Every new skill they learned in technology was a positive enhancement for their teaching, both online and in their regular classrooms. They found it very exhilarating to create their courses in a different medium and enjoyed the challenges of mentoring online students. Being involved in an online program gave some teachers the extra little lift they sometimes needed to rejuvenate what they teach everyday. It was a challenge to teachers to try getting a project across to students who weren't sitting right in front of them. These teachers with experience also know what works with students in their classes, so they aren't just shooting in the dark when they create online assignments.

What will most likely work best will be a mix of teachers with strong skills in technology and in designing lessons. If you have teachers with great capabilities in both areas, they are your best bets. As long as a teacher is open to learning new technology, however, he or she shouldn't be discounted from the program because of a lack of technology skills.

Strong communication skills are essential for all online teachers. Communication is the name of the game in online schools. The teacher must be able to write lessons in a way that students can easily understand. If the teachers aren't good at written communication, the students quickly get lost within the courses and do not fully understand how to complete their assignments.

Also in the realm of communication skills are the abilities of a teacher to communicate with students through e-mail or online chats. This type of communication is totally different from face-to-face communication in classrooms. In a class, both students and teachers can read the body language and intonations of speech to help them decipher meaning. This isn't true with online communications. Teachers need to be able to convey concern, interest, and willingness to help students without using any visual clues. They can't be short and to the point in written communications because the message may be misunderstood as mean and uncaring. Jokes in a classroom may come off just fine but the same jokes online may hurt feelings or just not appear funny.

We have found that online communications with students can be a rich and rewarding experience for both the student and the teacher. It is very personal and can make the students feel that the teacher is taking a personal interest in their education. In a classroom of thirty or more students, the students don't interact regularly with the teacher. Sometimes students can sit in classes and never talk at all because they choose not to engage in what is going on or because they are too shy to speak up in class. Online communications offer the shy student or the student with learning difficulties the opportunity to ask questions without the glaring eyes of fellow students. Online communications offer a safe way for students to get the necessary information to understand and complete lessons. Students often get to know their online teachers better in a more one-on-one way than they do the teachers they see at school. The teachers also find that online communication allows them to individualize the instructional interaction with students.

Another proficiency closely linked to communication is organizational skill. Without the ability to organize an online course, a teacher struggles with helping students understand where they should be and what they should be working on. If students can't look at a course online and almost intuitively navigate through it, then the teacher hasn't done a very good job of designing the course. The best of lessons won't work online if students don't know how to get to them or find any supplementary materials to use with those lessons.

You can have a teacher with all the technology, curriculum/lesson creation, and communication skills needed to be a successful online teacher, but if he or she doesn't have passion for the project, you will have a staff of lackluster teachers, and it will show in your program. If I was looking for one thing when I was interviewing teachers to work on creating our online program, it was passion. These teachers are called upon to step out of the box as they figure out how to get complex concepts through to students from a distance. They are asked to spend many hours creating from scratch a program and courses that didn't exist before they create them. They are asked to become more personal with students than they ever may have been before. They need to work together as a team to find areas of weaknesses and brainstorm ways to turn those weaknesses around. Ultimately, this means that teachers must come into the program with passion for the project. Teachers need to show enthusiasm for this new and uncharted delivery method in teaching in K–12 schools.

If a teacher interviews for a position and shows any hesitancy toward his or her own ability to create courses online, he or she is likely to continue looking for all the reasons why it won't work instead of looking for ways to make it work. You don't need naysayers within your online program because you probably have enough of them outside your program. You need teachers working from within your program who can be cheerleaders for it and can spread the word in a positive way about what you are trying to accomplish. You also have a lot of work to accomplish together, and having to constantly deal with negative influences can be very draining on everyone.

I discovered that the teachers who were excited about this new way of teaching and learning found the whole creation process to be an educational experience that stretched their skills in both technology and curriculum development. On the other hand, teachers who seemed to want to create courses for the monetary benefits often didn't enjoy the process. They were more combative when times got tough and often wanted to be compensated when any little bumps caused them any extra effort or time. This reinforced my decision to hire teachers with passion. If you don't have at least some teachers with passion, success will be hard to come by. You do have to temper the passion with compensation for all the extra work and creative energies put into the program, but merely throwing money at people to create an innovative project is doomed from the start. Like students, teachers do not have true passion for learning unless they have intrinsic motivation for it. Money is an extrinsic motivator. Although it's important to compensate teachers fairly for their work, you do not get quality courses and have quality mentoring for students by throwing money at the teachers. The exceptional teachers have an internal desire and commitment to the program and to their online students. These teachers create quality lessons at any cost and strive to improve what they originally created without being prodded into it by directives from a supervisor or by monetary rewards.

OTHER PROGRAM-RELATED STAFF

The secretary for your online program needs to be a versatile individual. When you are starting a program from scratch, all people involved end up wearing many hats. It is like starting up a home business where people are doing whatever needs to be done and are learning as they go. Your secretary will most often be the first line of contact with people interested in your program. You need someone who is very helpful and knowledgeable about the program. Students, parents, and teachers in our program know they can call our secretary with silly questions or any concerns and she will help them get the answers they need. She makes them all feel comfortable, which is important when we don't see everyone on a regular basis. Every communication needs to be positive and done in a tone of caring and concern. Equally important is to train your secretary in the technical side of the program. The secretary will get a lion's share of all requests for assistance, and if he or she can handle the request right away, your program will appear much more service oriented.

A counselor to help parents and students plan their studies is important when you have high school students involved in your online program. The online counselor does the same kind of work that all counselors do at schools. He or she helps students plan their schedules, helps them look at post–high school options, gets them graduation and testing information, and makes contact when students seem to be struggling. We found that sometimes students working on school from home didn't spend the time they should on coursework. Our counselor makes calls and checks up on students. If they are struggling with issues preventing them from getting coursework done, the counselor tries to assist the students in coming up with a plan to get back on track. It is invaluable to have someone within your online program staff who can look at all the graduation requirements and assist students with making decisions about their futures. The day-to-day connections that a casual phone call from your counselor makes to the students can be the one thing that keeps the students engaged in the program. They know we haven't just signed them up and left them to flounder through the program on their own.

A person who deals with technical support working for an online program is mandatory. You need to have someone who can set up computer systems for teachers and students. This person is the one who can troubleshoot technical problems with any computers or peripheral equipment. It is amazing how you can send out computers, which are all the same model and have all the same software, and you can have the variety of technical support issues that come up each and every day. With a technical expert on staff, you have a person who knows your systems, and this makes troubleshooting easy and effective. If a teacher's or student's computer is down, he or she isn't able to go to school. This is a major issue when your whole program is online. Students and teachers are at the mercy of the technology, and few things are more frustrating to people than not getting their computer problems dealt with quickly and efficiently. The way your staff deals with the technical support issue can make or break your program. When students get frustrated, they can drop the program just out of frustration even though they tell you it was too hard and the technology was too difficult to figure out. It also helps if everyone in the offices who might answer a phone has the technical skills to troubleshoot the more common problems that seem to come up. Having quick (and correct) answers to problems keeps everybody up and running and ultimately content with the program.

Another staff member who is very helpful to an online program is a teacher/trainer who is available during the regular school day. All of our creation and mentoring teachers work in regular schools during the school day. They aren't instantly available to students when questions arise. Students can e-mail them and often get answers within a couple hours, but when the problem comes up, the students may have to move on to something else until they get an answer from their online instructor. With a teacher on staff during the school day, students have another avenue to get answers to immediate problems or questions. This teacher plans and conducts orientation sessions to train both parents and students to use your online courses before the school year begins. This teacher individually trains students who enter your program after the initial enrollment time. Often, people go home and start to use the online site and find they need extra assistance navigating the courses. The teacher can schedule times during the day to have individuals come in for additional training and assistance until they feel comfortable doing it on their own. We have a minilab of eight computers in our offices so that students can drop in and get some assistance from our staff or just have a quiet, structured place to work. We found that some students need a place to get some help organizing their workday or need time away from a noisy house that isn't conducive to learning.

OTHER DISTRICT STAFF

Although we have some staff who work daily in the online program, we often tap into other district staff for assistance in their areas of expertise. Online teaching is not a self-contained home business—it is part of a large school organization. Because of this, we are able to tap into different departments to get needed assistance in specific areas. Our main support person is our deputy superintendent who promotes the online program and is our point man for communications with state officials and board members. This person can't dedicate a lot of time to the program because of his or her other district obligations but is invaluable in promoting the program. For this reason, it is important to keep him or her informed and part of the decision-making process so that information is always current and accurate.

District principals at all grade levels and coordinators of curriculum departments are involved in planning our online program. Each has an area of expertise and a unique perspective and brings different issues to the table as we plan what our program will become. Having the opportunity to tap into their years of experience moves the planning along in a way that wouldn't be possible if planning only involved the online staff. Knowing who to call and what kinds of expertise everyone has is invaluable in getting quick answers to your questions. You need to have good working relations with almost every department in your district, as you will most likely need assistance from most of them as you create your online program.

Your district technology department (MIS) is invaluable to your online program. They are experts on networks, computers, troubleshooting, and so forth, and have the training to help you make good technology decisions. They are also your technical support person's back up. Your technical support person can't possibly know how to solve every problem that arises, so he or she may need to tap into the wealth of knowledge in your MIS department.

If you plan to write any grants to start up or continue your online program, your district's grant department is important to connect with. They know about a lot of federal and state initiatives that your online program might qualify for. They also are experts in writing the grants. If you write the grants yourself, it would be wise to at least ask the grant personnel to look over your grant before submitting it. They often know what granting agencies are looking for in grants that they fund.

Although your teachers may search for websites appropriate for their lessons, it is also nice to tap into the expertise of your district library media specialists. Our teachers gave the specialists topics for lessons, and the specialists did some online searching for age- and subject-appropriate sites. We also used an online service that provided the same services. Both the paid service and the free district specialists are good avenues for helping your teachers find good sites to add to online lessons. The teachers are very busy doing many things at once; reducing the large amount of time needed for searching and finding excellent sites is a welcome assistance. Our district also has a lending library in our Instructional Support Center, where our online offices are housed. Parents and students use the lending library to check out library materials for research projects or for leisure reading. The library staff in the center is always available to the families when they use the library.

Also housed in our support center are our campus support teachers. They are expert teachers who work with teachers in schools to perfect their craft. These campus support teachers work with our online program during attendance day by running learning centers, teaching lessons, and giving assessments. They also assist me during the year if I need help administering state and district assessments. If you have similar positions in your district, they will be invaluable in supporting your program. I even asked three of these teachers to edit courses once they were complete to check for content and grammar mistakes. It never hurts to get a different pair of eyes to look at courses. They also were able to check for ease of understanding of instructions. If these trained adults can't understand instructions, chances are the students won't either.

We provide access to our district's Parent Teacher Resource Center, which is housed in our support center. This is a place where district teachers come to create hands-on learning games and activities. We also allow parents of online students to use the center for similar purposes. The staff in the resource center train parents to use the laminators and die presses and show them how to construct projects. If your district doesn't have a resource center, you could provide the hands-on projects within your program if you feel it is something your parents would find beneficial.

To create brochures, flyers, catalogs, and other marketing materials, you may need the assistance of district's graphic designers, your marketing department, and your district's print shop. If you don't have some of these departments within your district, you may need to outsource these services. It was much cheaper for us to use the expertise of district staff in these areas when we created marketing materials. You need to work closely with these people to make sure you get the effect you are looking for in marketing your online program.

Our district video production department created a marketing and informational video of all the activities and elements in our online program. They spent the whole first year of operations videotaping all events and interviewing students, parents, and teachers involved in the program. At the end of the year, they edited the pieces together into a professional tape and DVD to promote the Wichita eSchool program.

You may have other district personnel to tap in to, and you should. Any and all expert assistance you can get will save you time trying to figure things out yourself. You can't do everything in-house, so don't even try. Know when you don't know something and get the expert help you need. If you find you are spending an inordinate amount of time dealing with one issue, chances are you don't have the background skills to get things done. Use your time instead to find and work with people who can deal with the issue and get things moving again.

6

PLANNING AN ONLINE PROGRAM

PLANNING TEAM

Planning and creating on online program from scratch will take approximately one school year. Start planning in the fall of the year before you plan to offer the online courses. Even though you may be overwhelmed by the amount of work required, if you give yourself and your staff more time to get things done, you will lower the stress levels of everyone involved. Initial planning sessions should involve key personnel from different departments within your district. Early input from different perspectives allows you to avoid problems later in the design process. You want to involve as many stakeholders as you can to get their perspectives and have everyone's input for meeting the needs of the end users, your students.

Our initial planning meetings included the Wichita eSchool administrative coordinator, the deputy superintendent, two assistant superintendents, principals at all levels, teachers, the fine arts director, the curriculum director, the professional development director, the marketing director, personnel in the grants department, the teachers' union president, the MIS chief operating officer, the sports director, the Title I director, the director of purchasing, and a campus support teacher. These were mainly people who could make decisions for their departments so that little time was wasted having meetings and then getting permission from directors down the line. If you get a group like this together, you don't want to waste their time. You need to have a tight agenda and some preliminary decisions made that you can share with the group and then ask for their suggestions to improve on initial ideas. Ask very specific questions of the directors and get commitments for support needed down the line.

Our first planning meeting agenda included only two main topics: marketing and teachers. We shared the marketing venues we planned to pursue, such as mailings, TV, and newspapers, our website, the home school newsletter, and a booth and presentation at a local teaching parents conference. The second meeting included topics such as the results of the teaching parents conference, pre-enrollment numbers, the web hosting contract with local service, selection of Blackboard as our e-learning platform, the number of teachers to hire and the criteria used when interviewing them, budget expenditures versus FTE state funding, and a preview of the board of education agenda item to get official permission to open the program in the fall.

Much of this had to be done simultaneously to have everything done by the following fall. As the coordinator of the program, you need to be involved in every area of the program's development. You need to be involved in all decisions being made, and then you need to make sure directors and coordinators in other district departments are kept up to speed so they don't feel out of the loop or, worse yet, get the wrong information.

TIMELINE FOR PLANNING

Early Fall

Early fall is when you have a lot of brainstorming sessions. You meet with the planning team and make some decisions about the vision, objectives, and intended audiences for your online program. Much work needs to be done between planning meetings to check on things brought up in previous meetings so you can come back to the group ready to share the information you have researched. This is also a good time to research other online programs by looking on the Internet, reading technology journals, attending technology conferences, and even calling coordinators in other programs to ask specific questions. Once the initial planning meetings are complete, the pace really picks up in the winter and spring months. It takes a lot of good timing to get everything done when it needs to be done. Just try to remember that you have many balls in the air at once and you need to check on them often to make sure things are getting done. You may think your requests to other departments are a priority, but others may not.

January

January is a time to make sure you are in line with any state guidelines for online programs. Deciding which classes you plan to create for the next fall needs to happen early in the winter. You also need to decide on any large purchases for services or technology equipment. These might include video production carts, online lesson software, online searching services, server service and technical support, and your e-learning platform. If you wait too much longer to make these decisions, you may have a hard time getting permission for the purchases from your board. It also takes time to research everything and shop for the best products and prices. Once you decide which products to go with, you will need time to negotiate and sign any annual contract or purchasing agreements.

If you are planning to distribute a catalog later in the year, now is the time to get started on gathering the information you want to include.

February

February is the time to get any presentations ready for your board of education. In order to request permission to purchase items for your program, make sure you present your current pre-enrollment numbers or other items that show the program is moving along and will be ready to go by fall. Every time you go before your board, you need to bring them updates and show any positive progress being made. They are much more likely to vote for and support spending money on a new program if they know you are on top of things and that all indications are that the program will be a success.

March

March is the perfect time to start hiring teachers for the program. You might think about a team of people to help you interview teachers so that you can get through all the interviews in a timely fashion. We got together as an interview team and decided on questions we would all ask. This way we could give every teacher a numeric score for each question and compare the results, even though different people interviewed them. To let teachers know about the positions, I had an informational meeting and used flyers and district e-mail to get the word out. During the meeting, I told the teachers what they would be doing to create online classes, when the two-week workshop would be, what the pay scale was, and any other pieces of information about the program they might be interested in knowing. One thing I never kept a secret was the fact that this would be a very involved project and that they would earn every bit of the money. It would take a lot of time and commitment on their parts. I also let them know that it was a work in progress and that we would make a lot of decisions as we went along. Nothing was set in stone, and we really had no roadmap to follow. We would be working in uncharted territory most of the time. If they were looking for a project where they could be creative and help make decisions, this was the project for them. If they wanted to sit back and have someone spoon-feed them everything a little at a time, this was definitely not the project for them. The teachers then had the opportunity to ask questions and find out if they thought creating and mentoring online classes was something they would be interested in pursuing. If they were interested, they could sign up to be interviewed. The way it worked for us, it was fairly easy to find those teachers who seemed to have a passion for the project versus those who were looking for quick money.

April

Purchasing and some marketing work need to be done in April. Now that the teachers have been hired, you need to purchase the computers, printers, scanners, software, and ISP service for their home workstations. You need to load software, take inventory, and check equipment out to teachers. As soon as the computers arrive and are loaded with software, you can get them into the teachers' homes. This way you don't have to store them, and it makes sense to get them in the teachers' hands as soon as possible. In April, you should also be putting together any brochures, flyers, or catalogs to market your program. Graphic designers need to finish their end of the marketing materials so you can get them to the printers in plenty of time to let people know about your new program. This is also the month that we put together an informational video to play on the district cable station and use for conferences.

May

The month of May is when you mail out your informational brochures or catalogs. You want to get the information out as the school year is ending so that you can plant the seed about the possibility of trying online classes. Because you have mailed informational materials, you will start to get calls, mailings, and e-mails from potential students. You need to have someone available to answer the mass of questions parents will have before they pre-enroll their children. Because your workshops for teachers are held in early June, you might have a preworkshop meeting to take care of miscellaneous information and questions that the newly hired online teachers might have.

June

June is creation time. This is when you have all your teachers spend two weeks together learning what they need to know to get started so they can then go home to finish their courses. This is also when they have quality time to plan together and make some group decisions about the look and feel of courses online. (See more about the workshop in the next chapter.) This is also the time of year that our local home school association has its annual conference, so we are busy preparing for and attending the conference to share information about our program and sign students up for the fall.

July

July is really the last date you can order any computers or other equipment and ensure delivery before the school year starts in August.

Textbooks that need to be ordered and picked up from your district warehousing area also need to be taken care of at this time. Any planning for enrollment forms that need to be ordered or created, procedures, staffing, and so forth should be planned by July. Your teachers should be well on their way to creating courses, but you might want to check up to see if things are getting done. If someone needs a little push or something is not working properly, now is the time to get in there and help the teachers solve the problems. You don't want someone to have to totally revamp his or her course after the fact. The teachers would much rather know early in the process that something needs to be fixed or redone; in the long run, it will save them a lot of time. No matter how busy you may be, you need to regularly monitor teacher progress. If you don't, you might be oblivious to the problems a nonproductive teacher might be having. Once the student computers are delivered in late July, software and plug-ins will need to be installed and an inventory of everything needs to be done to prepare for enrollment time.

August

August is enrollment time in our district. Parents need to come in and fill out forms, pay textbook rental fees, and pick up books and computers if they are planning to borrow one for the school year. August is also when we bring in parents and students to our district support center to go through an orientation session with their mentor teachers. The teachers explain the expectations for their courses and navigate their courses to show parents and students where to locate different materials. Our first day of school is usually in late August, so this is the month that we open our doors and start teaching online. Lots of support will be needed during this time to help everyone log on and navigate through the courses. Quick and accurate answers are key at this point. You don't want to waste anyone's time for learning with navigation and technical issues.

The First School Year of Operation

During the first school year of operation, you will still be making a lot of decisions. Once you actually have students enrolled in your courses, you will have things that need to be altered, fixed, added to, or totally deleted altogether. The beauty of online courses is that you can make changes and additions to the courses on a daily basis. It isn't like creating a notebook or textbook and sending it to a printer, after which few changes can be made. This means that the courses are never truly finished. They can always be enhanced to improve the instruction and activities for the students.

During the first year, you may also be planning for expansions in your online program. If you are looking at adding grade levels or course titles, you start the whole planning process all over again. This time, it should be a little easier to make decisions and plan because you have been through the process before. You can learn from any mistakes made during the first year and improve the process for everyone involved. As soon as you start the first day of school, you are planning for the next fall. If you don't start right away, you will be pressed for time to create new courses and monitor progress of current teachers and students. You will have more on your plate because you are, in essence, a principal of a school and simultaneously an administrator planning for expansions in the program.

TEACHER WORKSHOP

PREWORKSHOP MEETING

Prior to the two-week teacher workshop, I had a preworkshop meeting with all the teachers hired to create online courses. The sooner you do this after hiring the teachers, the better it will be. Part of the reason for having this preworkshop meeting is to let the teachers know about things they can be doing daily to get things together for the workshop. The agenda for the meeting included introductions of teachers and the courses each would design, the concept that the project would be a team approach, a timeline for having ISP cable accounts set up in teachers' homes, and ideas on what things to collect and bring to the workshop.

Teachers were asked to think about and list their personal values because we would be creating our group values and norms during the workshop. They were also asked to start gathering lessons, units, and any ideas or projects they already used in their regular classes. They were told to collect documents like worksheets, project forms, research materials, websites, book titles, and any other materials they would like to include in their online courses. Teachers who had already used word processing to create their lessons were a step ahead of those who had handwritten plans. If teachers know ahead of time to start collecting these materials, it gives them a good chance to sort through what they currently use and perhaps even to start word processing lessons.

Teachers need to know during this preworkshop meeting what they can expect during the two-week workshop. They need to know that they will work six hours a day, five days a week, and that they will live and breathe creation of courses during the two-week period. I made sure that they all had their computers and other equipment set up and that the cable lines were installed in their homes before the workshop started. This way, as soon as they left the workshop for the day, they could continue to work from home. The preworkshop meeting is also an excellent time to answer questions.

TEACHER WORKSHOP

I planned the two-week workshop to start the first day of summer break. I wanted to give the teachers the whole summer to work on their courses, so the sooner I got them together and got them trained, the more time they had to create their courses. On the first day of the two-week workshop, I asked the teachers to brainstorm and share the values they each found important. We used Inspiration software to record the teachers' ideas and turn them into values and norms for our group; they came up with the work ethic that they believed everyone should to ad-here to while working together. Once we all agreed on the values and norms, they were printed and shared with everyone. There were several reasons we concentrated on this activity the first day. It sets the ground rules for our two weeks together, and it is a document that we could turn to when times got tough in order to pull the group back together. When everyone is doing what they should be doing, the document isn't really needed; when you have someone not pulling his or her weight or not fol-lowing set norms, the document helps to point out group promises to each other without getting personal about it.

After developing the group values and norms, it was time to move on to training the teachers to use all the hardware and software. This will actually take a lot of time. We had training sessions first thing each morning and left the afternoons for individual creation of courses. If you just trained teachers during the workshop and had them do practice types of activities, you would waste a good deal of time for creating their courses. Teachers should leave the workshop with a structure for their courses and parts of their courses already created. In other words, you must teach them something they need to know, then let them use the new skill right away.

The first thing the teachers need training on is the e-learning platform you have selected for your online program. I started by showing them what the students will see and how they will access materials online. Next, I showed them how to get into the back end (the teacher's portion) of the software to create lessons and add documents. One of the first items the teachers can then create that first day is the teacher contact information. They can take digital photos, upload the photos, type the contact information, and add any biographical information about themselves. These tasks are very simple, but it gives everyone a sense of accomplishment right away. This should not be a workshop where teachers feel frustrated that their time is being wasted. They need to get just enough information to go on with the next part of designing their courses. The whole workshop is built on the concept of just-in-time professional development.

Other training sessions included training teachers to use the scanners to scan documents, creating pdf documents with Adobe Acrobat software, use of Inspiration software for graphic organizer creation, and creating PowerPoint slideshows for use in video sessions. Teachers also need training to use the e-learning software to create online tests, quizzes and surveys and to use the online grade book.

In order to give the teachers the "student's" view of the course, I created an online course for the teachers. The course is on the same e-learning platform they are using to create courses, but the teachers are the students. I created Tegrity video sessions of all my training sessions. One video is how to navigate the front end (or student's view) of the e-learning courses online. Another video is how to use the back end (or the instructor's area for creating courses) to create and upload the course components. Separate videos are available on creating tests, quizzes, and surveys and how to use the grade book and look at course statistics. Still other videos show teachers how to create PowerPoint programs and use the scanners. The teachers can refer to the videos anytime and anywhere to get a refresher on the training they received in the workshop.

Before I created the instructors' course online, I had to field a lot of individual questions about little points teachers couldn't remember from the training sessions. Once the course was available to them, the questions on how to use all the software and equipment almost completely ceased. I also created a lot of how-to, step-by-step documents to assist teachers as they did some processes. These documents were added to the instructors' course so they would always have access to them. Rubrics for evaluating the structure and content of courses were also added to the instructors' course. These rubrics were introduced to the teachers early in the workshop so they would be aware of the criteria used to evaluate their courses. Another section of the instructors' course is technical support. This area has all the technical support contact information they need for the software and hardware used in the program. Often, the teachers need to call or e-mail the tech support people themselves to talk through the problems they are having with the software or hardware. The instructors' course is a catchall for anything and everything the teachers may need to create their courses. It will take time to put this course together, but it is well worth the effort. You can add documents or videos to the course as you add new software or equipment. The course can also be used every time you add teaching staff or new courses to your online program.

If you have software or hardware that you aren't able to train the teachers to use, you will need to outsource the training. This may mean finding someone within your district to do the training. It could also mean hiring a trainer from outside your district. Either way, you need to get people involved who can give the teachers the training they need in a very quick and concise way. If you are fumbling around trying to figure things out in front of the teachers, they won't have faith in what you are demonstrating. It is worth it to bring in some experts and get the training that really prepares the teachers to use the software and hardware effectively. I also found that some of the teachers hired to create courses had technology skills that were very helpful during the workshop. It was a great experience to see the teachers assisting each other to figure out new skills. Some of the teachers even conducted the morning training sessions for their colleagues. We also had a trainer from the video creation company Tegrity come to Wichita to train teachers to create videos. I wasn't an expert in using the video creation carts at the time of the workshop, so it saved us time and gave the teachers a better training experience by outsourcing their training. Each of them received a six-hour, hands-on training day with five other teachers. The trainer stayed for the whole first week of the workshop in order to train each and every teacher to create his or her own videos. Once the teachers received their training, they started to create the videos they wanted to use to lecture to students and give them visual instructions. Again, the teachers got the information and training they needed and then went directly to creating course videos. By the end of the summer, they had collectively created close to 400 instructional videos that students could view online.

During the workshop afternoons, teachers were involved in a lot of planning meetings. Planning meetings went in two directions. First, teachers in the same curriculum area would meet. They would discuss what items to include in courses, how they would move from one grade level to the next and not duplicate projects or research, and how they would all add assistance online for students to prepare them for state and district assessments. By planning together as a curriculum team, they could make sure that they followed a good scope and sequence. We didn't want to have all English teachers teaching the same novel titles or all social studies teachers researching the Civil War. Teachers would also meet with grade-level colleagues. These meetings would be used to plan for research or project activities that could be multidisciplinary in nature and avoid duplicating their efforts. When I looked at teacher comments concerning the two-week workshop experience, I found that the time to plan and make decisions together was one of the things they liked the most. They don't often get extended amounts of time to work and plan with colleagues, so it was an experience they all found unique about our workshop. The bonding that the teachers experienced during their planning meetings was what held them together as a group once they returned to their regular teaching jobs at district schools. They had become a team over the summer, and it kept them together even as they communicated from afar over the Internet.

When teachers weren't involved in planning meeting in the afternoons, they were busy working on the structure of their courses. Initially, each of them needed to decide how to structure his or her courses.

They needed to decide if they would create chapter, unit, or project areas. They needed to decide how students would access worksheets, videos, websites, and so forth for individual lessons. It takes some time to discover the structure that works best for a given course. Although the e-learning platform you use will dictate some of the structure, the teachers still have some individual decisions to make. If the structure a teacher chooses to use seems impossible for students to navigate through, you may need to step in and make some suggestions early in the workshop. Once some teachers start to create their structures, you can also use their courses as examples for other to get ideas. Sometimes, all a teacher needs to see is how someone else does something. You don't want to let any of the teachers struggle too long with structure issues, so you need to monitor courses from the very beginning. If they have to do some reworking, they may not be too thrilled; eventually, however, they will appreciate that the course is structured well and that they didn't have to redesign it once they had a lot of work already done.

Once you complete the first week of your workshop, it is a good idea to get feedback from the teachers to check that they are getting the training and help they need to create their courses. We just did a quick check with teachers listing pluses (the good things) and deltas (the changes) for the week. Then, based on feedback, you can make adjustments to give the teachers a better experience during week two. Get feedback at the end of week two as well so you can alter or enhance the workshop for teachers in the future.

By the end of the workshop, teachers should have started their courses and have the technical skills needed to continue creating their courses from home. From that point on, the only thing teachers had to do from our offices was create the online videos because they shared the three video carts. They may continue to call or e-mail to ask questions or get advice, but they should be independent by the end of the workshop.

You could have workshops after school or on Saturdays during the school year, but I believe that the bonding and total mind and body commitment to two solid weeks produced more product than training in short bursts over weeks could ever have accomplished. If it is at all possible, look for a two-week period to allow your teachers to learn, plan, and create together.

8

DESIGNING ONLINE COURSES

Once you have decided on the intended audience for your online program, you can move on to the elements you want to provide in the courses. If you are just using your online platform to enhance traditional classes at schools, you won't need to include specific lesson plans, answer keys, or lecture videos. You might include directions for projects, worksheets or forms needed to complete work, a calendar of due dates, field trips, or other housekeeping forms. If, on the other hand, you are looking to create a total school program online, you need to include many more elements. What you include online can be anything and everything that students use and access in a classroom.

COURSE INFORMATION

In our case, we were designing our courses online to be full courses that could be taught through online materials and done totally from home. The first item we made sure to include was a lot of informational material. We had an area in our online platform to include course information. This is where we put course syllabi so the teachers could share their course expectations and grading policies. This was also the area to include navigational forms to help students find items within the online course. Teachers provide charts of assignments and due dates for high school students and, in the case of K–8 students, the approximate timelines to finish courses in one school year. Something we added in the course information section was a video session of each teacher's course orientation. Teachers had their students attend face-to-face orientation sessions in our computer lab. When the teachers talked about how their courses would work online and showed students how to navigate in their courses, we used the Tegrity video carts to record their sessions. Then we uploaded the orientations to a server and added the link to the sessions in the course information area. This way any student who wanted to review the orientation session at home could do so any time. The orientation session is always available to students who enroll in the program after the orientation session takes place. This is the very first thing I tell all new students and parents to look at so they have an overview of the courses. Another item in the course information area is a folder that contains Wichita eSchool office information. It is a place to put information about upcoming field trips, forms for attendance, calendars for assessment dates, and so forth. This is where we place program-related informational documents.

CONTACT INFORMATION

The next area of our online courses is teacher contact information. In this area, teachers who mentor students can provide the students with contact information (e.g., e-mail address, phone numbers, and even a mailing address so students can mail assignments to teachers when they get in a pinch trying to hand in work). They can also provide a biography about themselves so students know a little bit more about who their teachers are and what they enjoy doing. We take a digital photo of all teachers during the workshop and add the photos to this area of the site. This allows the students to put a face to their online teachers. I also provide contact information for myself as the coordinator of the Wichita eSchool program. If the students or parents need to ask program questions, they can ask me or my secretary instead of the course teacher, who would need to get an answer from us and pass the reply on to the students.

COURSE DOCUMENTS

The course documents area is where teachers put documents that are not specific to one single lesson. They are items that will be used repeatedly throughout the course. Some items in this area could include maps of different regions and types for a social studies course, graphic organizers for an English course, math problem-solving processes, scoring rubrics in all curriculum areas, and scientific method forms for science courses. Students can open a map several times during the course and print out a fresh map for each assignment that needs that specific map. We also include any assessment preparation materials for courses in this area. These items might include directions to complete assessment tasks, lookalike assessments to practice skills, and rubrics used to score assessments. This is the same assessment information that would be available to any student at one of our brick-and-mortar schools. We want to make sure we provide the same experiences for our online students in preparing them for state and district assessments.

ASSIGNMENTS

The assignments area is where students go to get daily lessons, assignments, and projects for their courses. Teachers provide step-by-step written directions for lessons. They embed any documents or worksheets specific to the lessons right in the lesson folders. Students just select the assignment and print it out. Teachers also include websites to use for lessons within the assignments. This allows the students to go directly to the websites from the corresponding lessons on our site. Teachers have already done the web searching and found the appropriate sites for the assignments. This saves the students and their parents from using learning time to search for sites on their own. Students are given textbook reading assignments to complete within the lessons. They might have a worksheet to complete or a graphic organizer to fill out that corresponds to the lessons. Teachers, especially in math courses, often have Tegrity videos to lecture and demonstrate how to complete assignments included with written directions. They also sometimes provide helpful hints or guidance forms to assist students in completing assignments. Some of our newer district textbook adoptions include websites related to the textbook lessons. Students are often directed to the enhancements online to complete projects or assignments or even to take quick-check quizzes for specific lesson objectives. In our district's classrooms, we often aren't able to tap into these online enhancements on a regular basis, but in our online program, we can embed these sites right into daily assignments because we know the students have the technology they need to access the sites.

CALENDARS

We have a whole year of lessons for a course available to online students. Teachers provide daily assignment charts to help students organize their days and weeks and often add events to the course calendar to remind students of major course tests and state or district assessments. Students need as much guidance as possible to help keep them organized. We found in year one that when we let parents work at any speed they wanted, they were not very comfortable. They wanted us to lay out the timeline on a daily basis for them. We had shied away from dictating a timeline because we knew that every child working at home would be working at an individualized rate. We did add the timeline charts and let parents know that the timelines were just the average rate that student would need to complete the assignments. Their individual child would most likely be working above or below the timeline rate, depending on his or her interest and ability levels in each curriculum area.

BOOKS AND WEBSITES

The site also provides a separate area for books and websites. We looked at these separated areas as a place to put generic items. This area has lists of books related to the topics covered in the courses or leisure reading suggestions related to the courses. The websites could be used for research, extra practice, or enrichment activities. Teachers can package them together in folders for specific research projects. The students can then check out the suggested sites and use the ones they find appropriate for their research. Once again, the teachers do the advance preparation for the students and their parents so they don't waste learning time searching the Internet and trying to come up with age- and subject-appropriate sites that are valid and trustworthy. Teachers often also add just plain cool sites that they think students might be interested in trying out. We want to show students that learning online can be fun and engaging.

ONLINE GRADE BOOK

Our online e-learning platform includes an area to create online tests, quizzes, and surveys. Students can take the tests online and instantly receive their scores. Teachers embed tests into the assignments area of their courses. Students can then access their online grade book to see test and quiz scores. Our teachers also manually add the grades for daily assignments into the online grade book. This way students have a place to go to check their grades and see if they are missing any assignments. This area also helps the parents stay informed of their child's progress in courses on a daily basis. They don't need to contact the teacher or wait for midterm grades to check on student progress.

ANSWER KEYS

In our K–8 courses, parents are teaching on a daily basis and grading all work. For this reason, we also provide answer keys for all assignments. The parents have extra folders that have answers to textbook assignments, any worksheets or graphic organizers, and any scanned tests or quizzes that aren't in the online testing area. We don't provide these answer keys at the high school level because the high school program is designed for teachers to grade assignments online.

DESIGN CONSIDERATIONS

We created the above areas in our online courses, but this is by no means a complete list of items that might be added to an online course. You need to look at your specific audience and create courses that include the lessons and documents your students need to be successful in completing their assignments. Be aware that you need to be very specific about where to locate items and what students need to do to complete assignments. You really can't give them too much information. Because a teacher isn't right there in the room with them to answer little questions that always seem to come up, you cannot be vague about what you want students to do. You need to provide guidance in a step-by-step format so students don't get lost along the way. At the same time, make sure students know they can contact the teachers to get added information or help understanding assignments at any time.

EVALUATING ONLINE COURSES

Once teachers have had time to create their online courses, you need to plan a day when they can get together to evaluate each other's courses. Everyone knows from the first day of the workshop how they will be evaluated because they are introduced to the rubrics at that time. As they work on their courses, they can refer back to the rubric to check that they have included all the elements asked of them. I used two different rubrics to evaluate the online courses. One rubric was used to evaluate the structure of the courses and the other to evaluate the actual content of the online courses.

COURSE STRUCTURE SCORING RUBRIC

The rubric for evaluating the structure of online courses is the course structure scoring rubric (see figure 9.1). I used the main areas of the Blackboard e-learning platform to assist me in creating this rubric. You should do the same with whichever e-learning platform you choose to use. The announcements, course information, staff information, course documents, external links, and assignments sections of the rubric relate to the platform areas we used to structure our online courses.

Area of course scored	Score of 1	Score of 2	Score of 3 Benchmark	Score of 4
Announcements used to bring attention to new items	Never used	Used sparingly	Available when needed	Used often and well to bring attention to new items in course
Course information includes a course syllabus, information about structure of online course, and helpful hints	No course information supplied	Includes a very brief outline of the course and very few informational details	Includes a course syllabus, grading policies (high school), structure/navigation information for the course	Includes all the items in a score of 3 and extra helpful hints. Very detailed and informative
Staff information includes teacher biography, contact information, and photo	Only name and e-mail provided	Very basic contact information with office hours and email	Includes a teacher biography and all contact information needed by students and parents	All contact and biography information of teacher provided. Also includes photo and extras
Course documents are forms that are usable in many lessons throughout the course	No course documents	A few (2–3) documents are available	Course documents are appropriate for course needs. Directions for how to use documents and which lessons to use them with are provided.	Course documents are plentiful and include information for how to best use them is provided. Documents are also found in lessons that they fit into in assignments area.
Websites appropriate for use with course lessons	No external links provided. No	A few links (3–5) are course topics and directions to let user know where to use the sites	Links are appropriate for the organized in age of students. Links are organized in folders by topic. Directions for when to use links are provided.	Links are plentiful, folders, appropriate for students' age, and enrich the lessons within the course.

Figure 9.1.   Course Structure Scoring Rubric

Assignments Lessons and activities for the students	Assignments are very sparsely written and not well organized in folders.	Assignments are there but not organized well, lacks folders and that are easy to follow	Assignments are appropriate for the students. They are well organized in folders and directions are easy to follow.	Assignments are excellent. Extras abound. Organization is exemplary.
Proper conventions in spelling and grammar	Many errors in spelling and grammar, making assignments hard to follow	Some errors in spelling and grammar. Need to spell check more often before uploading lessons	Very few spelling and grammar errors. Easy to understand directions and follow them throughout the course.	Convention elements are exemplary.
Books	No books listed	A few books or journals are listed.	A variety of books and journals are listed that correlate with lessons.	A wide variety of required and related materials are provided with a bibliography as well as a description.
Instructions to parents and students	Instructions are often not included but instead are assumed.	Instructions are very broad and often hard to follow.	Instructions are easy to follow, and explanations are appropriate for the students' age level.	Instructions are excellent. The parents and students are given all the information they need to complete lessons. Details are often added.
Rollouts Deadlines for making lessons available each quarter	Never on time	A few assignments missing at rollout	All lessons and course information ready at rollouts	Ready before rollouts and continues to add extras after rollout occurs
Online assessments	Not provided	A few major tests (units tests)	Use of online testing is done for chapters, units, and projects	Use of online testing goes beyond major units/chapters.
Mentoring online Parent/student contact	Never initiates contact with parents/ students.	E-mails seldom and very brief with replies. The mentor never initiates contact with parents/students.	E-mails often. Initiates contact with students/parents on a regular basis. Doesn't just wait for parents/students to ask questions.	Goes beyond expectations in contacts with parents/ students. Goes into detail when answering

Figure 9.1. continued on next page

			relationship with parents/students.	parents concerns.
Tegrity sessions Use of video in course	No Tegrity sessions in course	Very few Tegrity sessions to supplement course	Use of Tegrity sessions to introduce new concepts and demonstrate information	Instructor goes beyond expectations of Tegrity sessions to introduce new concepts

Area of course scored	Score of 1 Poor Quality	Score of 2 Below Average	Score of 3 Benchmark	Score of 4 Exemplary
Announcements				
Course information				
Staff information				
Course documents				
Websites				
Assignments				
Proper conventions				
Books				
Instructions				
Rollouts				
Online assessments				
Mentoring online				
Tegrity sessions				

Teacher: _____

Person Evaluating Course: _____

Course Title: _____

Course Number: _____

Figure 9.1.   (continued)

A score of 1 on the rubric means that nothing has been created in that area. A score of 2 on the rubric means that a little bit of work has been done in this section but not enough to have a quality course. A score of 3, which is the benchmark score, means that the teacher has included enough information in this area so that students can easily navigate through and use the course materials. A score of 4 is exemplary and means that the teacher has gone above and beyond the benchmark and really enhanced the course.

Other areas are evaluated using this rubric. Grammar and spelling conventions are checked as well as a list of standards taught in all lessons. Instructions for lessons are written in a way that students can easily complete tasks. Answer keys are provided as part of the kindergarten through eighth-grade courses. Extension activities are provided, and online assessments correlate to units and chapters studied by students. The teacher's ability to meet rollout deadlines and how engaged the teacher is in mentoring the students are also evaluated in this rubric.

COURSE CONTENT RUBRIC FOR LESSONS

The second scoring rubric is the course content rubric for lessons (see figure 9.2). This rubric goes a little deeper than the structure of the courses and looks at the lessons themselves. The teachers are scored on creating a course syllabus that outlines the course and their expectations for students. They also need to define the communications requirements for both the teacher and the students. Students need to know up front what to expect and what they need to do. These elements of an online course are the same kinds of information that teachers share with students during the first days in a new course at school. The rubric also asks the high school teachers to define deadlines for handing in work and what criteria will be used to evaluate the work. The middle school teachers are evaluated for the answer keys they provide to parents who grade daily work at the middle school level. All lessons need to have introductions, a list of standards, a timeline for completing work, materials needed to do the assignments, directions that are direct and easy to follow, activities that allow students the opportunity to practice new skills, assessments to evaluate progress, and extension or reteaching activities. All areas on the rubric are scored with a four-point scoring scale, with 3 being the benchmark score.

Course content area to scored	Score of 1	Score of 2	Score of 3 Benchmark	Score of 4
Syllabus or outline of course	No syllabus or outline of course	A very sketchy syllabus or outline	A detailed syllabus or outline provided	Very thorough syllabus or outline provided
Communication expectations	No communication expectations	Sketchy communication information	Detailed communication information is provided.	Teacher provides an extensive list of communication options.
Evaluation of work **High school	No evaluation information	Very little evaluation information	Evaluation information is detailed and easy to understand.	Evaluation information goes into great detail.
Answer keys **Middle school	No answer keys	A few answer keys—not enough to grade all work	Answer keys for all assignments	Answer keys go into great detail.
Deadlines or due dates **High school	No information on due dates	Very little information on due dates	Due dates policy explained and easy to understand	Goes into great detail to explain due dates for assignments
Introduction for lessons	No introductions	Seldom uses introductions	Uses introductions in most lessons	Always has introductions that spark student interest in lesson
Standards correlation	No standards	Lists a few standards	Standards correlated to lessons	Standards abound in lessons
Timeline	No timeline	Few lessons timeline	Most lessons have timeline	Timeline always provided
Materials	No materials lists	Few materials listed	Lessons always have materials listed	Materials list provided and substitute items suggested
Directions	Directions not detailed and don't make sense	Directions very brief and not always clear	Directions give enough detail and are clear	Directions go into great detail and are crystal clear
Student practice	Activities not appropiate for lesson taught or lack any variety	Activities don't vary much and are not very interesting	Activities appropiate for objectives of lesson and uses a variety	Student assignments are exemplary and plentiful

Figure 9.2. Course Content Rubric for Lessons

Assessments	No assessments	A few assessments for major assignments	Both scanned and online assessments for daily lessons/chapters/units	An abundance of assessments are available to check progress.
Extensions and reteaching	No extra extensions	A few extension activities	A wide variety of extension and reteaching activities	Extensions are exemplar and plentiful.

Course Content Areas	Score of 1 Poor Quality	Score of 2 Below Average	Score of 3 Benchmark	Score of 4 Exemplary
Syllabus or outline of course				
Communication expectations				
Evaluation of work **High school				
Answer keys **Middle school				
Deadlines or due dates **High school				
Introduction for lessons				
Standards correlation				
Timeline				
Materials				
Directions				
Student practice				
Assessments				
Extensions and reteaching				

Teacher: _____ Person Evaluating Course: _____

Course Title: _____ Course Number: _____

Figure 9.2. (continued)

EVALUATING ONLINE COURSES

I use both rubrics to evaluate every course myself before I bring all the teachers together to score each other's courses. I pair teachers in the same curriculum area to trade courses, evaluate each other's courses, and give rubric scores. While they are evaluating each other, I ask them to sit with me and go over my rubric scores for their courses. I do this rubric scoring a few weeks before the courses will be available to students. You want to be able to make suggestions and let teachers know where they have areas of deficits that need to be fixed or added to so they can make the little changes or additions before the students are online and notice the missing items.

It was amazing to watch the teachers interact as they evaluated each other's courses. They really looked at the evaluation time as a time to give constructive criticisms and get ideas for their own courses. Many of them left the session ready to add elements that they had never considered. Sometimes it helped to see how someone else laid out a course to spur on new and creative elements in their own courses. Everyone looked at the evaluation session as a learning experience, and no one took it as harsh criticism. This happened because they all trusted each other and me at this point in the process. I would not have subjected them to outside evaluators coming in and telling them what was wrong with their courses. It needed to be people in our inner circle who critiqued the courses.

10

MENTORING ONLINE STUDENTS

A very important element in providing students with lessons and activities online is the mentoring support from the teachers who design the courses. Without individualized online support to ask questions and get assistance, learning online can be very difficult for students. The kind of support mentors provide can be varied. I have the mentor teachers check their e-mail every day to see if students or parents have asked any questions. We promise twenty-four-hour turnaround for answering questions online. In most cases, the turnaround time is only a few hours. Students also know that teachers are not available during weekends or district holidays. The mentors are available to students on district in-service days, though, because the teachers are on contract on those days.

If mentors become ill or for any reason are not able to check and answer e-mails, they know to inform the office so we can change the site contact information to the office e-mail in order to answer the questions. We also e-mail all students in that course and let them know that the office is covering the e-mails until the mentor is able to take over again. Mentors also have logs they can use to track their e-mails. The logs give us information on identifying the most needy students and those who never make any contact.

I would suggest that you have your mentors make contact with students on a regular basis instead of just waiting to reply to students' e-mails. They should send a welcome e-mail the first day of school to say hello and let students know they are available. They should also contact students and parents right before state or district assessments to give them assistance and to remind them to come to the support center to take the assessments. If students aren't making any attempts to stay connected to the online mentors, the mentors may need to initiate e-mails and ask for specific replies to get the students engaged in communications. The mentors sometimes call students to help them with subjects they know the students are struggling with. I do ask the mentors to direct questions about the program to the office because their jobs are to answer questions related to their courses. I don't want them to worry about program issues.

ELEMENTARY AND MIDDLE SCHOOL MENTORS

At the elementary and middle school levels, the mentors often interact with parents as well as students. They are asked what they might suggest for a student who is struggling with a certain topic or skill. Sometimes they want additional ideas for projects or books to read on a given topic. Mentor teachers sometimes even ask the middle school students to e-mail them with what prior knowledge they have on a topic before they start a new unit. If the student's prior knowledge seems lacking, the mentor might help him or her get up to speed or suggest extra materials to read or activities to try. The parents are the ones using the site at the elementary level, so very few e-mails come from the students. Once the students are in middle school, they are on the site just as much as their parents. Middle school was intended to be a transition from parents only during the elementary years to students only in high school.

HIGH SCHOOL MENTORS

At the high school level, the online mentors assign due dates for assignments in the courses. Students scan work or word process it and then attach the completed work to e-mails for their mentors. The mentors then grade all work and assign grades in the online grade books. The mentors at the high school level are full-fledged teachers to the students taking their courses; they aren't just helping home school parents put together lessons and assist them if needed. They are the ones assigning all work and giving the course grades. The mentors at the middle and high school levels come to the district support center to give any face-to-face state or district assessments. The high school mentors also give face-to-face semester finals for their online courses.

Connections with the online students are vital. The students who feel like the online mentors are really trying to help them and care about their progress do a lot better at staying on task and getting assignments to their teachers. The students who seem to have no connection with their mentors don't seem to stay with the program schedule or get assignments in when they are due. Some of these disconnected students didn't have a work ethic to get things done when they attended regular schools either. The online program was an attempt on their part to find a way to get through courses because they weren't successful when attending regular classes. These students find that it is much harder to find your way around an online course and take control of how much time you spend working on assignments. It is easier to go to school and have a teacher hand them assignments a day at a time and collect assignments at the end of the hour.

GRADE LEVELS

In designing online courses for students, we found that teachers at each grade level needed their own way to create courses and mentor students. Elementary grades (kindergarten through fifth grade) were the first grades we created online. We knew that it was too much to create a K–12 online program in just one year. We also knew that it was a good idea to start with the younger home school population. Once they were involved in the program, we could grow with the students so that in year two, the students who had been in fifth grade during the first year were needing the middle school courses by the second year. We also knew that high school courses would have the most issues to discuss and solve in order to offer full high school credits for the online courses.

ELEMENTARY

In regular elementary schools, students have one teacher for all academic subject areas. The only time they usually see other teachers is when they go to physical education, music, or art classes. To design all the core subjects in the online program, we used two teachers at each grade level. These teams of two split up the subjects and designed lessons and activities. If you plan to use more than one person to create courses for a grade and have them share the creation work, I would suggest that you do not have the teachers share a subject area. Most of our teachers each took whole subjects to design on their own, but in a few cases we tried to split a subject where one teacher took the odd-numbered chapters and the other teacher took the even-numbered chapters. Each teacher wrote the lessons from their chapters in the textbook and designed any other related activities for the areas of study in their chapters. The problem with this design is that one of the teachers is most likely more innovative with activities or is more thorough in writing directions. Parents and students notice the difference and wonder why some topics and chapters seem lacking compared to others. I also found that the teachers had a harder time sharing a subject area; one teacher often found fault with the other or blamed the other when things weren't done in the course. It worked a lot better to divide up each subject area and have each teacher design everything in his or her subject areas.

The subject areas that we designed lessons for in the elementary online program included math, science, health, social studies, and language arts. The language arts courses include reading and writing skills lessons, grammar practice, and lots of related leisure-reading activities and other projects and activities to teach language skills. We did not include separate courses for art, physical education, or music, even though many of the lessons included art activities. If students in our online program want to take these other classes, we allow them to take them in one of our neighborhood schools. They sometimes sign up to take library, music, physical education, or art classes at district schools. They can choose the classes they are interested in taking at a school, except that we don't let the students take core subjects at schools in combination with the online program. They are only free to take the non–core subjects at schools. This was a policy for our program because we didn't want to disrupt classrooms with students who drop in. The elementary teachers don't always teach every subject at the same time each day, and drop-in attendance would have been impossible to schedule.

Kindergarten courses are created completely differently from the first through fifth grade courses. The kindergarten teachers who created online kindergarten lessons use themes to teach in their regular classrooms. They also incorporated the theme approach to their online courses. They had daily activities like calendar and weather lessons, as well as language arts, math, science, and social studies lessons in each themed unit. Each unit includes enough activities to do lessons for one or two weeks. If the unit theme is apples, all lessons incorporate apples into them. Parents know which themes are coming up and can prepare materials or buy supplies at the store before their children are ready for the new theme. With the apples theme, they would buy apples for sorting, counting, making apple prints, and so forth. In total, we have thirty different themes for kindergarten students. Some of the themes are fire safety, dinosaurs, eggs, friendship, and famous Americans. The parents find this a really fun way to work on skills for their kindergarten students. The teachers supply many patterns and hands-on activities for small children to cut and color. They also provide websites for young children that correlate to themes, suggest library books to read following the themes, and even provide certificates of completion incorporating the themes.

We designed our K–5 programs for home school families. We provide all the lessons, textbooks, related websites, enrichment activities, and reteaching practice on the site. Parents also have access to answer keys for all lessons. Parents use the site to teach their children, and we offer as much assistance as we can. We found that some home school parents have a great program set up for their children. Others don't really know how to go about the business of teaching, although this is what they are attempting to do. We probably aren't needed for the first group of parents. We are very much needed by the second group of parents. They find it reassuring that they have lessons designed by teachers to work on at home each day. They also have the knowledge that their children are working on the same kinds of lessons as other children at their grade levels. They can see the standards being taught at each grade and know their children are on grade level with their peers.

One benefit for parents of doing the courses online is that they can move their children a grade level above or below in just one subject area if needed. Many times, the parents are home schooling their children because the children are working above or below the average pace in classrooms. After some assessments are given in the fall, we find that parents combine what they are seeing at home with the test scores to alter the grade level in a subject area. They don't want their children to struggle with reading lessons at a higher level if they can move them back a grade in reading and pick up skills that are lacking. This is very easy to do online. All we have to do is change the course in the course lists online and switch out the textbooks. Sometimes students work at a lower grade level for part of a year, and then by spring they may be ready to go ahead and start lessons at their regular grade level. What we are able to do is individualize learning for each student in the program. Within each lesson are reteaching, regular practice, and enrichment activities. By doing this, we provide activities for students who need more teaching in a subject, regular practice for on-target students, and enrichment activities for advanced students. Parents simply need to know that they shouldn't do all three levels of activities for lessons; they need only select the one level that is appropriate for their child. Because we have activities for all types of ability levels, the courses are often overwhelming to parents. It takes parents a while to adjust to the variety of options incorporated into each lesson. These are the same options that teachers make every day in classes for students.

When elementary teachers mentor the courses for elementary students, they are communicating with the parents of students. Our online courses are not designed for kindergarten students to access the site and find their own lessons. The site is designed for parents to access lessons and support materials. Students spend their time working with hands-on activities often printed out from the site. The students do use the computers at times to go to related websites to play learning games or do other age-appropriate activities. The parents use the mentors to ask questions about their children's progress, get advice for areas where the children might be struggling, or just to have someone to be in contact with. The mentors are a support system for the teaching parents. The mentors also supply the teaching parents with a calendar for completing assignments. The calendar is nothing more than a basic outline of what should be done each week to complete the courses following a standard school-year timeline. The parents may find that their children don't follow the calendar assignment dates exactly, but they have the calendar charts to assist them in planning daily activities.

MIDDLE SCHOOL

Middle school was designed during the second creation year. Four teachers were hired to create core middle school courses at each grade level. The core courses are math, language arts, science, and social studies. Each teacher designed one course for the students in the grade level, so each student has four mentor teachers during each of the three years. The courses were designed to incorporate district textbooks and all the activities and lessons that the teachers use in their regular classes. Students in the middle school level may also work at different grades for different subjects. Some students are able to work a grade level above their grade in one or two subject areas; some need to work in a curriculum area at a grade level below their assigned grade.

We designed the middle school courses a little differently from the elementary courses. At this level, the home school parents are still the teachers on a daily basis, but students are able to access the online site themselves and find their assignments. We created two courses that are a mirror of each other, with one exception: the parents' courses have all the answer key folders and the students' courses do not. The parents have four courses that we enroll them in. They have their own user names and passwords to access their courses. The students don't have access to these courses so they don't have access to the answer keys. The students are enrolled in copies of the parent courses and have their own user names and passwords. The students use their student courses to take any online tests that will show up in the online grade book. The parents do not take any online tests, and the grade book is not used for their courses. We feel that it is important for the middle school students to start to learn how to navigate through the online courses so they are prepared to work in courses on their own when they move on to high school courses. The middle school years are the transition years where parents are still involved but students start to take more responsibility for their own learning.

At the middle school level, each subject area teacher is an expert in his or her field, so the students have mentors who are able to answer subject-specific questions. The mentors at this level receive e-mails from parents and students because they are both navigating through and using the online site. The parents are the full-time teachers of students at this level. They must keep a grade book on their own and decide when the students are ready to move on to new units of study. The mentors are there to assist the parents as needed, just like at the elementary level.

We plan to add elective courses at the middle school level during year three or four. We will add six middle school elective courses: art, health/fitness, music appreciation, computer applications, keyboarding, and Spanish. The students will be able to select two elective courses to take each year along with their four core courses. The students may select two electives each year, one elective, or none at all. If the student wants to play an instrument or sing, he or she will still have to attend a district school for those courses.

HIGH SCHOOL

High school courses were designed during the second year of creation and took a different turn from those at the elementary and middle school levels. Once students enroll in high school courses, they are working directly with the online teacher mentors for each course. The teachers are accredited by the state of Kansas to teach the courses online. This means we can give the students who pass the courses fully accredited credits toward graduation. The courses created in our online program are just as rigorous as those attended at our regular high schools. We have other programs within the district for students looking to complete high school with a GED or other lesser credentials. These online courses are the same courses with the same course numbers and names as their equivalent classes at district schools.

We decided to initially create only core courses for students at the high school level: World History, U.S. History I, U.S. History II, Government, Sociology, English I, English II, English III, English Composition and College Reading, Biology, Physical Science, Earth/Space Science, Chemistry, Pre-Algebra, Algebra I, Geometry, Algebra II, and Pre-Calculus/Trigonometry. A student can't graduate from the online program because we only offer seventeen courses at this time, and the high school students in our district need twenty-two credits to graduate. If the students are planning to graduate, they need to attend one of our district high schools for elective courses to supplement the courses they take online. For most students, the electives they take are physical education, art, foreign language, music, drama, and drivers' education courses. Students can be dual enrolled. They take the core courses online and attend regular schools for their electives. During the third year, we will add core courses that we found were lacking in the program during the first high school year: science survey, informal geometry, world literature, and English composition. Electives in Spanish, art, computer applications, family and consumer science, and other courses that lend themselves to being taught online will be added in year four. Not all high school courses will transfer to the online environment. Drivers' education will always need to be taken face-to-face at a school.

The teachers who design the high school courses decide on all required assignments that students need to complete and hand in for credit. They design assignment charts that lay out what needs to be completed for each unit of study or chapter in a book. They provide all the supplemental forms and worksheets and incorporate websites and teacher instruction videos. Some activities are in the courses for extra practice and aren't handed in for credit. The students in high school check out a scanner from our program if they don't have one at home to use. They can scan handwritten assignments common in math courses and on worksheets where they print out the worksheet on which they write answers. Because the only ways to get these types of items to teachers are to scan, fax, hand deliver, or snail mail them, we chose to use the scanners. Sometimes the students come into our offices to deliver stacks of assignments that we then pass on to teachers through district mail. Students may also mail assignments to teachers if they fall behind in scanning work.

Students at the high school level are no longer working hand-in-hand with their parents as at the elementary and middle school levels. Parents are asked to check on student progress and make sure assignments are being done. The students are working directly with the online teachers to get credit for their coursework. If they have questions or need more instructions to complete assignments, they contact the online teacher for assistance. Because there is a timeline involved in preparing for and taking semester finals, the high school courses are not as flexible as the other two age levels where parents and students work at their own pace. Students come into the Instructional Support Center each semester to take semester finals for all their online courses. Although they are getting credit for daily assignments, they can't pass online courses if they fail the face-to-face finals. We take students work on an honor system online. We assume that the student enrolled in the course did the work handed in. We can't check that this is in fact the truth, but neither can teachers in a regular school setting. Every time students leave a classroom to finish an assignment at home, theoretically they could have someone else do the work for them. Some people try to tell me that online courses are just allowing students to cheat. I believe they are not allowed any more opportunities to cheat than any classroom in America. If students were to hand in work done by someone else at a school or online and then attempt to pass the course final, they would be setting themselves up for failure. Once students receive a passing grade for any of the online courses, the grades are put on a transcript and can be transferred to any high school if they move out of the area or decide to attend a school. When high school students have accumulated all twenty-two credits they need to graduate, we transfer their online credits to the district high schools they attended for electives, and the high schools grant their diplomas.

SPECIAL EDUCATION AND OTHER EDUCATION ISSUES

Our online program is not set up to handle the many needs of special education students at any of our age levels. If a student has special education needs, we suggest to parents that they attend one of our brick-and-mortar schools where special education teachers and curriculum are available. Our online program is just that, a program; as such, it doesn't need to provide every service that would be required if it were a school. The only thing we can do in our program is offer the opportunity to have a student work at a different pace than in a regular classroom at the elementary or middle school levels.

We can also provide a way to keep a student learning even though he or she may have medical issues. Many students with illnesses go through times when they feel well and other times when they are too ill to do any work. Working online is a convenient way to assist these students. They can do a lot of work and even work ahead during times of wellness and slack off a little when they can't deal with schoolwork. They also have the availability of course materials twenty-four hours a day, seven days a week, which means a student who is feeling well late into the evening can go ahead and work because the materials and directions are right there.

Pregnant girls and new mothers also find online courses to be helpful in continuing their education. Pregnant girls may not feel well enough to attend school every day, and they can fall behind. They fall further behind when they give birth and are on maternity leave from school. When pregnant girls enroll in our program, we work with them to plan their time around both their health and their coursework. The girls know they will be missing some time once their babies are born, so they often work ahead. We have also found that the girls get back to online courses quicker than they might be able to if they went to a school. Their coursework is right in their homes, so that when their newborns are sleeping, they can work on their coursework. Often the responsibilities of having to care for a child prevent these students from getting to school regularly. Through online courses, these girls can continue to get an education and spend time caring for their babies.

Although you can't be everything for everyone, you may find that students you hadn't even thought of serving will find your program and want to enroll. You need to look at each and every case individually and make a decision as to whether your program will benefit the student. Sometimes the answer will be no. In that case, we always make a point of trying to point the students toward the program or school that will meet their needs. You will do a real disservice to students if you enroll them in your online program and they don't get the education they need.

⑫

ENROLLMENT

PRE-ENROLLMENT

Pre-enrollment for your online program should begin just as soon as you are able to get marketing information out to your intended audience. You may as well get the pre-enrollments going, even though everything may not be complete. Creation will most likely continue up until your start-up date, so you really can't wait until you have dotted every *i* and crossed every *t*. Pre-enrollment will give you an idea early on as to the interest in the community for your program. If you have very few pre-enrollments, you will know that you may need to change your marketing approaches or add another audience you hadn't even considered in the beginning.

A website with an online pre-enrollment form is a great way to get information out to an audience. You can answer lots of questions, explain how the program works, and provide a place for parents to sign their kids up. Once you receive online pre-enrollments, be sure to make contact with the students or parents to let them know you did in fact receive their online pre-enrollment. You can do this through mailing postcards, replying to them through e-mail, or calling on the phone. We find that sometimes the phone call is best because we often learn more about the student than was asked on the online form. Sometimes the parents think our program will meet their child's needs but, in talking with them, we find that they were misinformed. It is always better to find something like that out right away so the parents can find another program that will meet their child's needs. Parents may also pre-enroll in our program by mailing back to us the forms that we include in our mailing catalog (see figures 12.1 and 12.2).

OFFICIAL ENROLLMENT

Once parents have pre-enrolled students and we have checked to see that the match is appropriate between what our program can offer and the needs and learning style of the students, the parents may officially

Student's last name: _____

Student's first name: _____

Student's age by August 31, 2003: _____ Birthday: _____

Teaching parent's name: _____

School district you live in: USD # _____ Phone: _____

Street Address: _____

City: _____ State: _____ Zip Code: _____

E-mail Address: _____

Use a district computer & printer: ____Yes ____ No, using own computer

Grade level for 2003–04 school year: *(circle one grade)*   6   7   8

It is suggested that a student take all their courses in the grade level they enroll in for the year, but there are some instances where a student may need to take a course in one subject area that is a grade level above or below their grade level enrollment. Please circle the grade level this student will be working at in each subject area below:

Language Arts   Science
6   7   8   6   7   8

Mathematics   Social Studies
6   7   8   6   7   8

Return this form to:
Wichita eSchool
412 S. Main
Wichita KS 67202

Figure 12.1.   Middle School Pre-Enrollment Form

Tenth grade online	1st Semester Courses	Course #	Credit	Check here to enroll	2nd Semester Courses	Course #	Credit	Check here to enroll
	English 2	1221	0.5		English 2	1222	0.5	
	Geometry	2421	0.5			2422	0.5	
	U.S. History 1	3361	0.5			3362	0.5	
	Physical Science General	4811	0.5		Physical Science General	4812	0.5	
	Subtotal online credit		2.0		Subtotal online credit		2.0	
Tenth grade electives (at a site)								
elective ?			0.5				0.5	
elective ?			0.5				0.5	
elective ?								
elective ?								
	Subtotal electives		1.0		Subtotal electives		1.0	
					Total credits		6.0	

Select the courses the student plans to take in the chart above. For electives please write on the lines provided courses the student is interested in taking and we will make arrangements for enrollment at one of our high school buildings.

Student's last name: _____
Student's first name: _____
Student's age by August 31, 2003: _____ Birthday: _____
Parent's Name: _____
School district you live in: USD # _____ Phone: _____
Street Address: _____
City: _____ State: _____ Zip Code: _____
E-mail Address: _____
Use a district computer _____Yes (must be enrolled in at least 3 courses)
_____ No (using own computer)

Return this form to: **Wichita eSchool**
              412 S. Main
              Wichita KS 67202

Figure 12.2.   Tenth-Grade Pre-Enrollment Form
**NOTE: Electives only needed if the student is working toward a Wichita Public School diploma.

enroll their students. As much as you may want high numbers of students enrolled in your online program, you need to look at what the program can do for each individual child. Your program can't be everything to everyone, and if you enroll students who don't fit the program, their chances for success are remote.

It works best if you can designate an official enrollment time and ask all parents to come to your building to fill out enrollment forms and pick up any textbooks and computer equipment. Our parents fill out many of the same generic enrollment forms that all parents in our district fill out at their respective grade levels. These include pupil information forms, Internet agreements, no tolerance for violence and drugs agreements, language surveys, and so forth. We also have parents sign forms to check out textbooks, novels, science kits, and computer equipment. All of these forms state that the parents are responsible for replacement costs if any of these items are lost, stolen, or damaged.

Parents who enroll their children sign a parents' agreement (see figure 12.3) for participating in the online program. The agreement states all the expectations for the parents and lists the responsibilities of the online program. In the parents' section, it states that an adult will instruct the student in the home and will be responsible for all learning activities, grading, attendance, and progress tracking for the student at the elementary and middle school levels. We provide all the lessons and related support materials to achieve this requirement, but because we cannot actually teach the students on a daily basis, we felt it was important to state this fact in the agreement. We can't be held responsible for what the student does or does not learn when we do not have control over the teaching experience within each household. The agreement also lets the parents know they are to provide their own Internet services within their homes. In order to participate in the online program, they must incur the costs of the Internet service. The agreement spells out any attendance times that students will need to come to our offices for activities or assessments. It also lets parents know that they are to read and respond when necessary to all communications and keep us informed of any address, phone, or e-mail changes so that communications can remain open. Other points in the agreement spell out that parents are to inform us of any equipment problems and are responsible for

Parents' Responsibilities

- Provide a teacher/adult to instruct the student at home and be responsible for student's learning activities, grading, attendance, and progress at the elementary and middle school levels.
- Provide and pay for an Internet Service Provider (ISP) connection to the Internet for access to online lessons.
- Teaching parent and student attend Attendance Day September 20, 2003 (8 AM to 3 PM) 412. S. Main, Wichita, Kansas.
- Student will attend all state and district assessment sessions at the JFISC (412 S. Main) as appropriate for their grade level.
- Read all announcements/calendar items so you stay up-to-date with events and activities.
- Read all e-mail from Wichita eSchool staff and reply when requested in a timely manner.
- Notify us immediately if you have problems with the computer or printer.
- Only access online accounts for students enrolled in the program; sharing passwords is prohibited.
- Malicious use of the network and damage to software components of the computer or computing system is prohibited. You will be responsible for damages.
- Use of the network to transmit material likely to be offensive or objectionable to recipients is prohibited (i.e., hate mail, harassment, discriminatory remarks, flaming, slamming, and other inappropriate activities). See usage policy P1232 (enclosed in this mailing).
- No illegal installation of copyrighted software for use on USD 259 computers.
- Family is responsible for any computer/printer that is lost or stolen while in their home.
- Notify Wichita eSchool when your child is no longer enrolled in our program and return all textbooks, computer, and printer to JFISC (412 S. Main).

As the teaching parent or guardian of _____, I have read the Wichita eSchool Parents' Agreement. I hereby accept all responsibilities as the home school parent in Wichita eSchool

Signature of parent: _____ Date: _____

Wichita eSchool Responsibilities

- Provide a teacher online who assigns all work, grades assignments, and assigns grades for online courses at the high school level.
- Provide online curriculum, aligned with state and district standards, for use in the home by teaching parents and students at the elementary and middle school levels.
- Provide each family of students enrolled in three or more courses with a computer and printer to access online lessons.
- Provide initial computer training to use the online site.
- Provide rental textbooks for all courses.
- Provide access to our secure online website through user names and passwords.
- Provide online support by certified teachers for parents and students.
- Provide state and district level assessments for all students at JFISC (412 S. Main).
- Provide access information for technical support for computers that need repairs under a three-year extended warranty.

Figure 12.3. Parents' Agreement

any malicious damage or stolen equipment. We also point out that sharing of access passwords to the online site is prohibited. If they have friends or family who want to join our program, they are more than welcome to enroll and get their own access information.

The program's responsibilities include providing teachers to assign and grade all work at the high school level and all lessons, support materials, and certified mentor teacher online assistance for the elementary and middle school level students. The online program provides rental textbooks and computers for students enrolled in three or more courses and provides orientation training to help parents and students use the site, as well as technical support for equipment when needed. The program also provides all the state and district assessments appropriate for each grade level.

It is important to have some kind of parent agreement so that parents are aware up front what their responsibilities are and what the program promises to provide for them. You don't want the parents to assume anything that isn't part of what you can provide in your program. By having parents read and sign the agreement at enrollment, you can avoid a lot of confusion later about everyone's responsibilities. Parents hear things when you explain them but may interpret them in their own ways. By putting everything down on paper, you can help make everything a little bit clearer. Your parents' agreement is a document that should be looked at each year to see if new items or issues have come up that might be important to add or change. You want this agreement to reflect the current program as closely as possible.

⓭

ORIENTATION FOR STUDENTS

When students enroll in the online courses during the summer en-rollment time, they should be given a time to come to a face-to-face ori-entation session. This session gives the students and the online teachers an opportunity to meet and get to know each other. Because they need to be communicating with their online mentor teacher throughout the year, it is nice if students and their parents can put a face with all those e-mails. We invite both the parents and the students to attend the ori-entations because the students will be accessing the site from home and could probably use another person in their homes who can navigate the site. During the orientation, the teachers show students how to navigate through their courses and explain how they designed the flow of folders and assignments. They also go over their course syllabi and explain what they expect of the students. Showing students where to access the as-signment charts and how to hand in work is also important to go over during the orientation. This is the time when the teacher can share ex-pectations and the students can ask questions.

At every orientation, we create a teaching video using our Tegrity video carts. When the teachers introduce themselves, go through their syllabi, and navigate through their online courses, the whole meeting is caught on video. We add this orientation video to the course information section of each online course. This allows the students to review everything said during the orientation. There is a lot of information for students to absorb during the two-hour orientations, so having a permanent backup to access at any time from home as a review is invaluable. The orientation videos also serve another purpose. Some students enroll after the official enrollment and orientation days. The orientation videos built right into the courses allow those new students to hear the orientation just like the students who were able to attend. This saves you and your staff a lot of time when you enroll new students throughout the school year.

We would find it almost impossible to start students in online courses without these orientation options. You need to establish some sort of orientation sessions, either online or in person, to help show students where to find things and get the right activities for the lessons. At first, the students need time to learn how to navigate through the courses. It would be a good idea to not just jump in the first week with a full caseload of assignments. It is better to have the student complete treasure hunting types of activities to find different parts of the courses and send the teachers evidence of success in doing so. Examples might be:

- Go to the animal website listed on this page and find three interesting facts to share with the online teacher.
- Go to the instructor information area and find three facts about your online teacher. Then click the teacher's e-mail address in that area and send him or her three interesting facts about yourself.
- Open the history worksheet, print it out, fill in the blanks, scan it, and attach the scan to an e-mail to send to your teacher.

All of these activities are meant to get students started using all the areas of the courses, to print out worksheets, to scan finished work, and to attach assignments to e-mails. All of these activities will be used to successfully complete courses, so giving students short practice assignments to check on everyone's abilities to do them correctly will be invaluable. If you give the students a week of adjustment time up front, you will be able to find glitches early on and help students correctly use the courses components. The time spent at the beginning pays off later when you do want students to not only navigate the courses but complete regular assignments on a daily basis and get them handed in to their online teachers.

(14)

FACE-TO-FACE OPPORTUNITIES

Our program is intended to be used online, but we feel that some face-to-face interactions among students and between students and teachers add value to the program. We therefore built many face-to-face opportunities into our online program. We found that every time we have students meet the teachers and each other in person, they leave the experience more connected to the program and to us. Even the teachers walk away from the face-to-face experiences more connected to the students. The face-to-face opportunities allow students to practice some of the oral presentation skills they need to meet state and district standards. They are also able to share visual projects with each other and have hands-on learning experiences we aren't able to offer online. To enhance your online program, it is a good idea to find opportunities where students and teachers can come together to interact.

ATTENDANCE DAY

Once students are enrolled in an online program and attend an orientation session to learn how to use and navigate the online site, they are ready to get to work online. Other opportunities present themselves to have students interact in face-to-face situations. One of those opportunities for our online program in Kansas is the state attendance day. This is the day the state counts students in attendance in all state schools to allocate per-student funds to support each school district. This is a day that all our students from kindergarteners to seniors come to our Instructional Support Center for a day of learning opportunities. We start the day by administering state and district assessments that are given in all our district schools in the early fall. These include the Metropolitan Achievement Test for third through eighth grade students, the Jerry Johns reading inventory for second grade students, and the DIAL kindergarten pretest. These tests give us a benchmark score for students' achievement levels. We can then use the assessments to monitor student progress in the program.

Once assessments are completed in the morning, the students are engaged in learning activities with their online teachers the rest of the day. The students and teachers get a chance to introduce themselves to each other. They also get a chance to do some hands-on and oral activities. These might include using microscopes in biology, bringing and sharing an "all about me" collage, giving an oral report, doing hands-on art-related activities, using math manipulatives, and participating in teamwork types of activities. Many of these activities are difficult if not impossible to achieve online, so using face-to-face times to give the online students these experiences should be your goal.

TEACHER SESSIONS

Although our program is intended to be online, the teachers sometimes ask the students to come to the Instructional Support Center as a group to present a lesson to them. Attendance is not required, and these sessions are generally used to prepare students for upcoming assessments. The teachers don't want to assume that all the online students found and completed all the activities online that would prepare them for the assessments. We discovered that allowing students to see the format of assessments and to have an opportunity to practice look-alike assessments help the students feel more comfortable when they take the actual assessments. This, in turn, likely increases their assessment scores. The face-to-face sessions also allow the students to ask questions and learn from what other students are asking. These sessions are usually one hour to ninety minutes in length and are very well attended.

ASSESSMENTS

Students who join our online program are required to take all state and district assessments for their grade levels. For some grades, that means coming in for assessments about once a month for one- or two-day assessments in math, reading, writing, science, and social studies. For other grades, the students only take the Metropolitan Achievement Test on attendance day and aren't required to take any other assessments during the school year. We give the assessments to our online students during the same window of time that students in schools take their assessments. We use the exact same guidelines and time limits. This means that students often have to come in for assessments on two consecutive days and must therefore be close enough to Wichita to drive in to the city twice during a testing week. All parents know about this face-to-face time commitment when they enroll their students.

HIGH SCHOOL FINALS

Our high school students are required to take face-to-face finals to receive credit for any online courses. We allow the students to do all regular assignments for credit online and even take chapter and unit tests online. We have the face-to-face finals to verify that the work done online was in fact done by the student. If the student takes a final and fails it but had all A papers, assignments, and tests online, then chances are someone else was doing the work. Many people outside an online program may feel that online courses make it very easy for students to cheat. We have found that the students' grades in daily work are reflected in their grades for face-to-face finals. In Wichita eSchool, there has not been a single incidence of high grades for daily work and then

failing the finals. If students failed the finals, we found they also had failing grades for daily work.

Coming in for finals allowed the teachers to ask students to bring in
course notebooks for grading or for students to share a presentation
orally as part of their finals. These activities are often part of the finals
grades for students in our schools, and the face-to-face finals requirement allows the students to have the same experiences and opportunities. Students can hand in any assignments that they wanted to get credit
for in the courses. Teachers are able to conference with some students
during finals days and assist them in getting last minute critical assignments done before grades are figured.

FINE ARTS EXPERIENCES

We have a very active fine arts community in Wichita. They have subsi-
dized the participation of many students across our district in arts-
related activities. Wichita eSchool has had the opportunity to participate
in their arts program. Students in the online program are able to attend
theater productions throughout the year free of charge. We send out
e-mails and announcements on the site to let families know about plays
and concerts, and they sign up if they plan to attend. The students and
their parents meet at the theater, and we hand out their tickets. They get
to attend young children's plays, Christmas plays, symphonies, and dra-
matic plays or musicals for older students.

Through the same community organization, we are also able to provide hands-on workshops for students with local artisans. Some of the
workshops include papermaking, water paints, storytelling, percussion
music, and creating quilts. Our students met regularly with a local quilt
artisan last winter to design and create a Wichita eSchool quilt, which
hangs in our office. The students love the chance to get together for fun
and creative activities. It is a good idea to find enjoyable, hands-on activities and field trip experiences for your online students. It gives the
students and program personnel an opportunity to get together for
activities other than just taking tests and assessments. You need to build
in some face-to-face experiences that allow everyone to be relaxed and
enjoy themselves. If you only see each other for high-stakes testing, you

won't have the positive relationships that are possible by also offering activities just for the sake of having fun.

OTHER ACTIVITIES

Our parents found that one of the online fathers was able to teach sign language. They organized sign language classes in the evenings for both students and parents. This kind of activity brings everyone together and offers some value to our program. They also started a bowling league team for the home school students in our program. This is another place for the students to get together, have fun, and get some physical activity. You should definitely tap into the skills and talents of your students and parents to find situations and activities to bring them together. Any and all of these activities will enhance your online program.

END-OF-YEAR OPEN HOUSE

At the end of every school year, we have an open house with cake and punch to celebrate the year. We hand out graduation certificates to kindergarten, fifth, and eighth grade students. We also recognize seniors who will be graduating at one of our high schools during the month of May. We ask students to bring in projects they have completed during the school year to share with everyone at the open house, and we have an area set up to display their work. These projects can be science experiments, research they have conducted, poetry or stories they have written, art projects they have done, or any other learning projects they would like to share. During the open house, people can walk through the display area and the students explain what they did and answer any questions viewers might have. This gives the students an authentic audience for projects they have completed at home. It also allows the students to practice their presentation skills.

Families are encouraged to invite friends and other family members to come to the open house to view projects or to learn more about the online program. We also mail out open house invitations to home school families in the seven-county area around Wichita. These families are invited to come see the students' projects and to hear about the online program and ask questions. This is a very effective way to provide information and share what students accomplish in the program. The new people also have current families to visit with and can ask them questions about the program to get an end user's perspective. This is a great way to open up your online program to the community. It is a good idea to let your local news people know about the open house, as they are always looking for a new community interest and education story. We found that the open house was one of our strongest marketing events to generate new enrollments for the next year. The open house is not only a celebration of the current year but also the first step toward enrollment for the next year.

15

OTHER SERVICES

Wichita eSchool is an online program, but it is a hybrid of other services, too. We offer many little services and opportunities that add value to what we provide online. Your district may not have the same services we have, but all districts have services that would be very easy to offer to online students. These services are greatly appreciated by families and show your commitment to helping their children get an education.

LIBRARY RESOURCE CENTER

Our district has a central lending library from which that all schools can borrow books. This allows teachers to collect more materials for research projects than are available in their own schools' libraries. This lending library is located in the same building as our Wichita eSchool offices, so it is very convenient for students and parents to check out books and other materials, such as listening tapes and kits, when they come in to our offices for other activities. Our online students conduct the same research as students in our brick-and-mortar schools, so they need access to the same research materials. It is also a great place for students and parents to check out leisure reading material. If you don't have a central lending library, you could make school libraries available to the online students or work with your local public library to provide specialized programs. Public libraries often design and teach sessions to students to help them use libraries and learn report writing and research skills. You need to pursue these types of collaborations and then let your families know about the opportunities and services.

PARENT TEACHER RESOURCE CENTER

Also housed in our Instructional Support Center is our Parent Teacher Resource Center. This is where both parents and students can come to create hands-on learning activities and wall charts for students. There are a variety of creation materials, including laminators, die presses of letters and shapes, stickers, folders, game movers, markers, posters, and so forth, to create all types of learning tools, games, and posters that a teacher or parent might want to use in a classroom or at home. Staff members in the center work with groups of our online parents to train them to use the center at the beginning of each school year. District teachers frequently use the center to make things for their classrooms. Our parents also love the opportunity to make learning activities for their students to use at home.

If your district doesn't have a permanent resource center that your online families could tap into, you can always offer miniworkshops on selected dates to have parents construct learning activities to help them teach at home or organize their home school efforts. Teachers do these kinds of projects every year. You just need to gather supplies and have a teacher provide his or her expertise in constructing the charts, posters, or games. You could even have the students themselves help in creating the projects they will later use at home. Our families liked the opportunity to come to a central location to construct as well as purchase school-related supplies that can sometimes be hard to find at stores. Our prices are also often a lot cheaper than commercial sources because we can buy in bulk.

PARENTS' SUPPORT GROUP

Our first-year parents wanted the opportunity to get together with new first-year parents in subsequent years and provide moral and logistical support. These parents came to me and asked if I could provide a meeting room on a monthly basis in the support center. They would provide the leadership and plan agendas for the meeting. You can't ask for more than parents who want to help each other. The first-year parents showed the new parents how to use the support services at the center and even planned creation times in the center for the support group to work together to create activities. They discussed topics like how to motivate their children, how to minimize household distractions, and how to deal with the stress of teaching many grade levels at once for multichildren families. They also planned the sign language classes, bowling league, and end-of-year picnic event.

While parents are in the support group meetings, we provide two services for their children. Their preschool-age children are watched in the center's daycare center. Their school-age children attend a workshop sponsored by the Arts Partners organizations. This way, parents can come to the meetings and all their children are being taken care of. It also reduces the number of times a parent would need to come to the center for student activities and for meetings because we combine their activities on the same days.

The parents run their support group. I don't plan their agendas. They do that by finding out the needs of the group. I do try to pop in to meetings and answer any questions they may have for me about the program. You can't make parents create or attend a support group. It really needs to come from them. If they see the need, they will come together to help one another. This group has been a real support to the parents who sometimes feel isolated as they work at home daily to educate their children. This support group is a great place for them to decompress and share successes.

eLAB

After the fall orientation in the center's large teaching computer lab, we discovered that we had times when we needed a few online computers. This brought about the establishment of the eLab. We have eight networked computers in our Wichita eSchool offices. The eLab is used exclusively by the students and parents in the online program. When we have new students who enroll after the fall orientation, we provide some hands-on training to learn how to navigate and use the online courses. Students can also view the orientation videos from the fall session at home after the training to refresh them on where to find things online. We also find that after training sometimes parents and students need quick little help sessions to get going. They can call us and come by a few minutes later to get assistance in the eLab.

Around midterm time, we found that some high school students weren't doing their daily work in a consistent manner, and their midterm grades reflected that fact. We sent midterm grades along with an invitation to attend an all-day training session. The session was mandatory for students who were failing to get them back on track, if possible. Those who did attend the daylong training session spent equal amounts of time working online in each of their courses. I wanted the students to see what a full six-hour school day online should look like. In many cases, these students thought that they could get online thirty minutes or less a day and somehow pass their classes. We watched to see if the students were struggling to navigate through their courses to find assignments and supplemental materials and to see if they knew how to scan work and send it as attachments to their online teachers. In many cases, they just needed help to use the technology in the ways they were intended to be used. I also spent time with the students to organize their workloads in each course. We printed out course assignment charts and checked off all assignments that were completed. Together we devised a process for the students to catch up with late assignments and continue to work on current assignments. After the day-long training sessions, the students were asked to check in once a week to show continued progress in their coursework. For some students, this was just what they needed to get organized and get work done on a regular basis. Once the students show they are back on track, they discontinue the check-in sessions. We found that some students got back on track and received passing grades by the end of the semester. Some of these students also continued to do weekly check-ins even after they were back on track because they found it to be a motivator to share their progress with us.

The eLab is also available to students whenever their computer equipment or Internet service isn't working at home. They can come and work so they don't fall behind because of technical difficulties. Students sometimes have noisy distractions at home and find that they can come to the eLab for some quality work time, if needed. We especially found this to be true of students with babies or very small children at home. To have a structured place and time to do schoolwork helped them stay on track.

We are always finding new uses for the eLab. If at all possible, your online program ought to have a few networked computers available for training or just to allow students a place to work where they have teachers to assist them. You need to have somewhere students can come just to print out a few assignments when their printers aren't working or Internet services get interrupted. This is important because when the equipment isn't working, school isn't available, and students can quickly fall behind.

ELECTIVES

As stated in earlier chapters, our online program allows students to enroll at a brick-and-mortar school for the elective courses we don't offer online. Students can enroll in physical education, drivers' education, art classes, vocal and instrumental music classes, and a myriad of other elective courses. The opportunity to enroll in electives while enrolled in our online program allows high school students to accumulate enough credit to graduate. We transfer all online credits to the schools where the students takes electives, and those schools provide the students with their high school diplomas. The electives allow students to be in courses where they interact with other students. They also get the opportunity to participate in courses that bring out their individual talents.

COUNSELING SERVICES

We have a counselor as part of the Wichita eSchool staff. She provides initial counseling, transcript reading, and suggested course selections for all high school students. This can get very complicated with home

school students. We have students with a wide variety of transcript and
course completion records because many home school students have
been in home school courses, private or religious schools, and even public schools. You need someone who has experience and knows the
course requirements in your district and has expertise in reading and
crediting courses from a variety of teaching institutions, including home
school records. The counselor is also available to get information to students concerning Work Keys, PSAT, SAT, ACT, and other tests that students may need to take for postsecondary education opportunities.
Counseling for college and university searching is also a service that a
counselor can provide for online students. Our counselor has been invaluable in making contact with students who seem to be struggling to
see if she can help get them back on track or to just hold their feet to
the fire to get assignments handed in.

SUPPORT SERVICES

No matter how small or how large your online program is, try to look for
opportunities and experiences for your online students. Many, if not
most, of the extras you can add to your online program won't take a lot
of your time or money, but they will all add value to your online program. You may not be able to look into all the different options you
could make available to your online students during the first year, but as
your program grows and you have more people on staff, you can devote
more time to extras that enhance your program. Even if our families
never take us up on all the activities and services we offer, they do appreciate that we offer them. Sometimes it is the smallest gestures that
show your families you are there for them and will help them in any way
you can. Many of the services may seem simplistic, but they show that
the program is trying to bridge the distance with many little connections, even though the students are at a distance. Once your core program is created, these extra services are well worth your time and effort.

16

ENHANCEMENTS AND IMPROVEMENTS

FEEDBACK

We are always getting feedback from parents and students about our online program and support services. They can easily send an e-mail to tell us that something in the site isn't working or let us know about a misspelled word. We are happy to get these daily feedback e-mails. It is easy to fix the little things they are having trouble with, and it shows that we are working to meet their needs on a daily basis. We have also used different means to gather feedback information in a more formal way to help us plan for and enhance the courses and the other services we offer.

Calls and E-mails

Every time we make contact with families, we try to find out if there is anything we can do to help them and ask if the online courses are going well. We gather a lot of vital information by doing this. At least a couple times a year, we make a point to call every student's home to ask how things are going, what is causing them trouble, and toward the end of the year, if they plan to enroll again the next school year. It is important to communicate and make connections as often as you can. Some of the information you gather will come in handy when you are looking at changes for the next year. E-mails are also a good means of connecting and communicating with families. We promise twenty-four-hour turnaround with e-mails, yet in most cases the e-mails are dealt with within hours of receiving them. This kind of quick reply to questions or problems shows your commitment to the students and their learning. Some of the really good ideas to enhance or fix our online courses have come from suggestions from families.

End-of-Year Survey

At the end of the first year, we created an online survey for families to help us as we went into the second year of creation and enhancement for the online program. The survey included scalable answers and explanations for those responses. Some of the questions were:

- The lessons are arranged in a way that is easy to follow.
- The assessments are a good way to assess my student's progress.
- The teacher who mentors our family online has been helpful.
- The eSchool office staff is available and helpful.
- My child has benefited from being involved in the Wichita eSchool program.
- The Parent Teacher Resource Center is an asset to the eSchool program.
- We plan to enroll in Wichita eSchool next year.

Once the survey participant answered the questions using a scale of answers ranging from strongly agree to strongly disagree, he or she could explain the answers provided. By doing this, we got not only percentages for responses but also specific information about those answers that helps us plan and create new courses or enhance current ones. This type of structured information is invaluable to you when you plan for the next year. Once the surveys were taken, the data from the surveys were analyzed so we could come up with findings and draw conclusions about the online program. Once we had these findings and conclusions, we were able to make recommendations for enhancements and fixes that were needed.

An action plan was then established to go through a process of using the information to make the necessary improvements. The action plan included sharing the results with all stakeholders. If you have a planning team, they will find the recommendations very useful as they plan for the future. Teachers in the online program and the students and parents they work with also want to hear the results of the survey and the recommendations taken from the collective data. Your board of education will need an end-of-year update as to the online program's success or lack of success. The survey is a great way to provide them with both qualitative and quantitative data. After the first year of operations, you could also share assessment results with your board, but I caution you to make sure your board knows that the initial assessments can only be used as benchmark data to then use in subsequent years to show growth by students after their initial year in the program. We also needed to make any arrangements to continue with any support services that the families felt were a benefit to the program. This may mean that you need to arrange for staff working in other departments in your district to continue working with your online students and parents. If you make any connections with agencies outside your school district to provide services, you can share results from the survey that deal with those agencies' services to help you decide if the services should be continued or enhanced.

Teacher Meetings

Another source of information and feedback concerning your online program are the mentor teachers' perspectives. They are the ones in the trenches every day, not only creating the online courses but also working online as mentors. They know what is working and what isn't, and each one has a unique way to handle teaching online. Getting your online teachers together throughout the school year to discuss successes and failures can give you a lot of useful information. The teachers often alter their courses on the fly as the needs arise, but it is good to get them talking about the changes they try so they can help each other develop courses that work for students. You can plan online courses, but you will never really know what works best until you get students and teachers online actually using the courses on a daily basis.

Then you can start to see the little things that you never would have thought of, no matter how long you had planned. The students seem to enjoy that they are part of the creation process, as some of their suggestions to teachers become changes in the courses. They feel like they are part of a living and breathing program that can be changed as needed to meet their needs.

ASSESSING THE ONLINE PROGRAM AND PLANNING FOR THE NEXT YEAR

Once you have gathered all the data needed to make informed decisions about the online program, you are ready to move into the second phase. This will involve almost as much planning as the initial year. Most likely, you didn't create every course or offer courses to all the audiences you would like to make online courses available to. Now you have one year of operations under your belt. You have hands-on experiences from both online teachers and students. You also have a wealth of information you didn't have when you first created an online program. Now comes the refining of the program and the enhancements that really make your online program what it should be.

Timeline for Year Two

Preparing for the second year online starts as soon as the first year ends. Throughout the school year, teachers may alter their courses as needed, but come summer they can revamp whole areas that they feel need major changes. Teachers who have already created courses for our program will spend the next summer and school year checking that websites they have in courses are still active for the second year. They need to be careful not to check them too early. If they check a site in August that won't be used until April, they may find that in April the site is inactive. The teachers may also use the summer to add new materials, make new teaching videos that they feel are needed to explain content to students, or delete materials that were not used or as helpful as they had thought. If a new textbook has been adopted for a course, the teachers need to redo the parts of their courses that use the textbooks.

They are compensated for the extra creation work they are required to do compared to teachers who only need to enhance their courses.

To add grade levels or additional courses to your online program for the second year means planning for those changes as early as late fall of the first year of operations. This means that you are trying to make it through your first year online at the same time you are trying to figure out what to add for the second year. You don't have the opportunity to get through an entire year before starting some of the planning that needs to be started for the next year. In our case, we decided to add middle and high school core courses in year two. By doing this, we would have core courses available for students from kindergarten to seniors. For our third year, we looked at offering our online courses to other schools within the state for a class fee. We also looked at offering the courses to current brick-and-mortar students as an option for students who carry full course loads and would like to try one online course. Another direction for us in year three was to look at which additional courses we wanted to add at the middle and high school levels. All of these different directions to take your online program involve much planning and creation time by everyone involved. By early spring, all initial planning and direction decisions need to be made. You need to add any new elements of your program to any marketing brochures or catalogs so they will be back from the print shop in time to invite community members to the end-of-year open house. By the time the open house takes place in May, you need to be able to provide information about what the online program will offer and what enhancements and services will be available for the next year.

By the first day of summer break, teachers should be hired and ready to attend the online workshop to prepare them to create new courses for fall. What is nice about the workshop after the first year is that the first-year teachers are now available to train the new teachers in the workshop. You now have teachers who have been in the trenches who can really tell them like it is. They don't pull any punches and are real mentors for the new teachers. It is just amazing to see how the new teachers learn from experienced mentor teachers. The learning curve is such that the new teachers can often avoid the mistakes the first-year teachers made. This allows the new online teachers to waste little time creating their courses in years two and three. They definitely benefit from the first-year teachers' experiences.

(17)

THINGS TO THINK ABOUT

Just when you think you are done, you will find that you have new things to consider and new directions to go. One thing I can tell you is always true with an online program: it will never be done. You will always be able to add to your program or fix and enhance what is currently there. An online course isn't a printed textbook that you have to keep using as is until you can afford to look at purchasing new textbooks some seven to ten years after the initial purchase.

In this chapter, I offer just a few of the items that have been thrown into the ring for our online staff to think about and sometimes act upon. These items are not meant to be an inclusive list, but instead are a list of ideas to get you thinking in different directions.

ONLINE CLASS SIZE

Initial Classes

When you first create online courses for students, you want students to sign up for the courses. Once the courses are implemented, you need to switch gears and decide how many students are too many. At some point, the number of students will become too much for the online teacher to handle. The problem with establishing one set number of students to enroll for all courses is that one number just won't work for all online courses.

If your teachers are only mentoring the parents who are doing the actual day-to-day teaching, as home school families do, the teachers can most likely handle up to fifty students in a class. These students and parents won't need daily assistance and will sometimes go weeks without hitting a snag. Once you move to the high school level and have the online teachers assigning and grading all coursework, you will find that the teachers most likely can't handle fifty students. Our teachers spend their regular school day already teaching a full caseload of students who also have coursework that needs grading on a daily basis. If your teachers mentor online courses as part of that regular schoolday caseload, they will be able to handle as many students as they would have in regular classes at school. If your online teachers only work with online students, they will be able to handle many more students than a teacher who mentors online as a supplemental job after regular school hours.

You also need to consider what kinds of assignments the students are given in different curriculum areas. Daily math assignments may be more time consuming to grade than another class where the students don't hand in assignments on a daily basis. Science courses like chemistry may require students to attend a few labs, so you will only be able to enroll enough students to fill the chemistry lab. You need to be flexible when you ask your teachers to keep track of time spent so they can help you find the perfect number of students for each of the online courses.

What to Do When You Have Course Overload

Once you are at the limit for a course, you come to a new decision point. Are you going to just close the course or are you going to do something to make room for the additional students? You could copy the original course and have another teacher mentor the exact same course. One problem with doing this is that the new teacher will never be as comfortable with the course as the creation teacher is. You could copy the original course and then give the new teacher some time to alter the course to include special units or projects that that teacher likes to use in his or her own classes. This way the new teacher has more ownership of the course. You do need to know ahead of time if you need an extra teacher, and that may be hard when students enroll close to the beginning of the school year. The final solution for adding an additional course for your overload of students would be to allow a new teacher to create his or her own course from scratch. This will definitely take the most time but will give the new teacher the most ownership in his or her course.

With each of these scenarios for adding new courses, you have different pay structures. The teacher who just uses a whole course created by someone else and mentors students would only receive mentoring pay. The teacher who uses a copied course but alters it to fit his or her own style and teaching activities would be paid a minicreation fee and mentoring pay. The teacher who creates a new course from scratch will need to be compensated for the whole creation fee and mentoring pay. Time also needs to be considered. Using someone else's course will take the least amount of time. Copying a course and making small changes will take a little more time, and the creation of a brand new course will take the longest. Quality of teaching is a final issue to consider in making this decision. Can a teacher do justice to a course he or she isn't familiar with and doesn't necessarily understand inside and out? Most likely, teachers manage courses they created themselves with more ownership and passion than ones that they are just borrowing. As you move away from the original creator of courses to teachers just using someone else's courses, you will most likely see a decrease in the quality of instruction.

CHANGING OR ALTERING YOUR AUDIENCE

You may select an audience for your online program originally but later find you want to add new audiences or even change your audience altogether. It is amazing how many different parents, students, and even other school district personnel will inquire about your program. With each new prospect, you hear of another audience of students for your program. The problem is that you can't be everything for everyone. If you don't have a lot of special education enhancements built into your online courses, then you shouldn't enroll special education students who won't have their needs meet. On the other hand, if you intended for your students online to only be home school students, you may find that homebound students or students who are new mothers may be inquiring about your courses. To alter, add, or change your audience will take some thought and planning. What needs to be changed or added, if anything, to meet the new audiences' needs? Some of the new audiences will be easy to add without doing much altering of courses. Some new audiences, like adding students attending other school districts, may take a lot of planning and changes in rules and regulations for enrolling. You may even need to get permission from your state department of education to forge these new partnerships. You are breaking barriers that until online courses came about were pretty entrenched in the educational system. What if you want to enroll students outside your state in your online program? From whom do you get permission and how will your homegrown courses work for a student thousands of miles away? If you require any face-to-face meetings, how can you alter the courses to allow students from a long distance to participate in them?

For every change or addition in audiences, you will have a myriad of things to think through and consider. To make changes in your audience, it is best to start thinking about the changes or addition in early winter so that you have time to brainstorm, make plans, get all the permissions you may need, and alter your courses (if needed) to meet the new audiences' needs.

TEACHER COMPENSATION IN CONTINUATION YEARS

You want to keep your online courses as up to date and current as you possibly can. This does not mean that you use courses year after year without any additions or enhancements. Some years, the textbooks and support materials are not going to change in curriculum areas. The teachers who created these courses should be compensated a portion of their creation fee to enhance their courses. If you pay teachers to create the courses originally and then just give them mentoring pay in subsequent years, you may see very little enhancement in courses. By paying the teachers to enhance their courses every year, you give them an incentive to bring their courses up to date. This keeps websites current and means that new activities and projects are added to improve and enhance the original courses.

Most likely you will find that every year some curriculum areas are adopting new textbooks. When this happens, you need to pay those teachers to revamp their courses to include the new textbook readings and assignments, new websites, and support materials. This won't mean that whole courses need to be totally recreated. Many parts of the original courses can still be used, but the teacher has more work to do to revamp a course than a teacher who is just enhancing. In the long run, all online teachers will have enhancement years and revamp years when new textbooks are added. This just means that the teachers' pay fluctuates from year to year.

TIME

Online programs bring lots of time-related issues to the forefront. From the start of your planning, you will need to consider time and how it will work in your online program. One time issue to think about is whether you provide online courses year-round or follow the regular school calendar. If you have year-round school, you will need to pay teachers and technical support staff to be available to assist students during the summer when by contract they are usually on vacation.

Online school can happen twenty-four hours a day, seven days a week—but do you want to have teachers and office staff also available to students during all that time? Will you have support and mentor hours when you guarantee a fast turnaround and other times that the students can work but the support won't be right there? Whatever you decide to do dealing with time issues, technical support, and teacher support, make sure you let the students and parents know what the calendar is and when help will be available. Nothing can be worse for your online program than to have students expecting a fast turnaround when they e-mail a request and later finding out that no one was available during the time they were waiting for an answer. If they are all informed about your hours and calendar, they will understand when no one gets back with them until after your district's spring break or other time when the teachers aren't on contract. You don't want anyone to feel ignored. That will only cause discontent, and some students may stop working if they feel no one is on the other end when they ask for assistance.

You could have your online program follow the regular school calendar and also include an online summer school session. If you are using the site year-round, be sure to build in time to recycle courses. This time is needed for any big system upgrades, to take students out of one year's courses and move them into the next year's courses, to delete students not returning, and to add new students for the new term. Your down time will be dependent on how many students you have, how many courses you have, and how long upgrades take in your e-learning platform.

Another time issue to take into account is seat time versus student learning. In most states, the students are tracked and promoted not by their learning but by how much time they spend in a seat attending school. In an online program, seat time takes a back seat to student learning. You can allow students to work at their own pace and continue to work on curriculum standards and objectives until they master them. This may be foreign to many people in your state departments, and it may take a concerted effort on your part to show them how it is student learning at the forefront in online school programs, not how many hours the students spend sitting at a desk in a classroom, that determines when the student is ready to move on to higher level courses.

FINAL WORDS

Now that you have read this book on how to create an online program, there is one more thing to do: just do it! You can read, search, and plan all you want, but ultimately it will never get done if you don't just take a leap of faith and start designing your online program today. Lots of things will stand in your way, but every one of them is surmountable. All you have to do is be very determined to make it happen, and it will.

ABOUT THE AUTHOR

Shawn Morris graduated from Wichita State University in 1984 with a bachelor's degree in education. She received a master's degree in library science from Emporia State University (Kansas) in 1996 and received a second master's degree from Wichita State University in educational administration in 2002.

Shawn has a varied background in education. She has been an elementary classroom teacher, middle school technology teacher, library media specialist, instructional technology specialist, and most recently, the administrative coordinator for Wichita Public School's online program, Wichita eSchool.

In connection with the online school program, Shawn writes articles for technology journals, is interviewed for articles on online learning, and presents the Wichita eSchool program at many national technology and education conferences.